COOKING FROM ABOVE
BAKING

COOKING FROM ABOVE
BAKING

MARIANNE MAGNIER-MORENO

PHOTOGRAPHY: FRÉDÉRIC LUCANO • STYLING: SONIA LUCANO

hamlyn

TO JÉROME

First published in France in 2007 under the title *La Pâtisserie*, by Hachette Livre (Marabout)

Photography by Frédéric Lucano
Styling by Sonia Lucano

An Hachette UK Company
www.hachette.co.uk

First published in Great Britain in 2009 by
Hamlyn, a division of Octopus Publishing Group Ltd
2–4 Heron Quays, London E14 4JP
www.octopusbooksusa.com

Distributed in the United States and Canada by
Hachette Book Group
237 Park Avenue, New York, NY 10017 USA

ISBN 978-0-600-61998-7

Printed and bound in Singapore

10 9 8 7 6 5 4 3 2 1

Measurements Standard level spoon measurements are used in all recipes.

Nuts This book includes dishes made with nuts and nut derivatives. It is advisable for those with known allergic reactions to nuts and nut derivatives and those who may be potentially vulnerable to these allergies, such as pregnant and nursing mothers, invalids, the elderly, babies, and children, to avoid dishes made with nuts and nut oils. It is also advisable to check the labels of preprepared ingredients for the possible inclusion of nut derivatives.

Eggs should be large unless otherwise stated. The Department of Health advises that eggs should not be consumed raw. This book contains dishes made with raw or lightly cooked eggs. It is advisable for more vulnerable people, such as pregnant and nursing mothers, invalids, the elderly, babies, and young children, to avoid uncooked or lightly cooked dishes made with eggs. Once prepared these dishes should be kept refrigerated and used promptly.

Milk should be full fat unless otherwise stated.

Butter is unsalted unless otherwise stated.

Ovens should be preheated to the specific temperature—if using a fan-assisted oven, follow manufacturer's instructions for adjusting the time and the temperature.

FOREWORD

I love baking but many times in the past it seemed that baking didn't like me... I strove to turn out well-risen, springy biscuits but they came out flat. I really tried to produce gorgeously textured chocolate mousse: it was too dense, or too dry. In the face of dozens of disappointments, made all the more frustrating because I followed the recipe instructions scrupulously, something nevertheless kept a spark of hope burning: in the midst of my flat biscuits, there was always one much higher than the rest; among my failed chocolate mousses, one of them seemed to murmur to me "You're on the right track." The right track maybe, but which one? The mousse stayed silent, the biscuit implacable. I felt as if I had met a brick wall.

In baking terms, this "wall" is all the books, recipes, classes, and workshops for both professionals and amateurs. In a nutshell, the wall of the novice baker is a huge ocean of advice and ideas—sometimes contradictory and often false—in which you have to immerse yourself in order to discover the hidden secrets. I dove in.

By picking my way, from equipment to frostings, I made it through the pastry-cook's maze. It meant copious note-taking, comparing, absorbing, and, above all, experimenting ceaselessly. From these discoveries, some principles were established and I never ignored the invaluable advice from top bakers. I learned, for example, the secret of chocolate mousse: the egg whites must be supple not firm if you want to fold them easily into chocolate; the chocolate-eggs-butter mixture must be warm and the egg whites must be at room temperature. Quite literally, I ran home to try it out. I hovered near the fridge for the required amount of time and, a few minutes before the specified time was up, I tasted chocolate mousse that was, finally, a success! For my biscuits, an American cookbook got me on the right route: the dough must be thick and the biscuits must be small (less than 2 inches) and the oven very hot (at least 450°F). Miraculously, my biscuits emerged from the oven tall and proud and—the ultimate test—crumbled into two under the slight pressure of my thumbs.

The book in your hands today is the product of copious effort, both patient and passionate. It has therefore for me a special worth, one that I hope you too will value once you have tried the recipes. My wish is of course that the results will be the finest baking in the French and Anglo-American traditions but above all, that it gives you that multitude of tiny details without which, in baking terms, there is no magic.

Marianne Magnier-Moreno

1

CREAMS & CO.

2

SIMPLE CAKES

3

LAYERED CAKES

4

LITTLE CAKES

5

TARTS

APPENDICES

GLOSSARY • TABLE OF CONTENTS

RECIPE INDEX • GENERAL INDEX

ACKNOWLEDGMENTS

CREAMS & CO.

CREAMS

Vanilla custard 01
Pastry cream 02
Butter cream 03
Almond cream 04
Lemon curd 05
Chocolate mousse 06
Chocolate ganache 07
Panna cotta 08

SAUCES & TOPPINGS

Caramel 09
Salty butter caramel sauce 10
Chocolate sauce 11
Red berry coulis 12
Red berry compôte 13
Chantilly cream 14
Plain frosting 15
Chocolate frosting 16

01

VANILLA CUSTARD

MAKES 14 FL OZ (ABOUT 1¾ CUPS) • PREPARATION: 15 MINUTES • COOKING: 15 MINUTES

1¼ cups milk
1 vanilla bean
3 egg yolks
⅓ cup sugar

IN ADVANCE:
Gently heat the milk in a pan with the vanilla bean split open and the seeds scraped out into the milk. Infuse (if possible for 10 minutes) then bring to a boil. Remove and discard the vanilla bean.

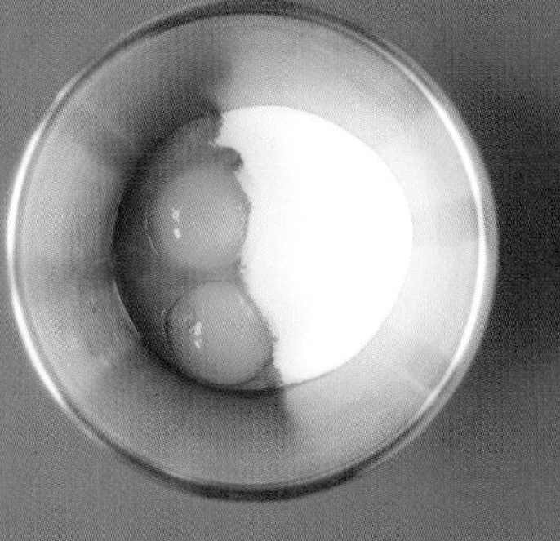

1 2

3 4

1	Put the egg yolks and sugar in a small bowl.	2	Beat them thoroughly until the mixture is lighter and has slightly thickened.	
3	Tip half the boiling milk in a thin steady stream onto the egg yolks while continuously beating the mixture.	4	Transfer the mixture back into the milk pan over a medium heat. Let thicken, stirring constantly.	➢

01

NOTE	TIP
☛ Make sure you scrape the base—especially at its edges—with a flexible spatula because that is where the temperature is highest and where the risk of coagulation of the egg yolks is greatest. The more the cream heats, the richer it will be, but there is a risk of it boiling and hence scrambling.	Watch the fine moussy trail that forms on the milk/egg mixture. When this mousse disappears, the custard is approaching 175°F, the temperature at which you must stop the cooking.

IS IT COOKED?	COOLING
Dip a wooden spoon in the custard then run your finger down the back of it: it should leave a clearly visible line. The custard is ready!	Pour the custard through a fine-mesh stainer over a bowl and let cool, stirring from time to time. Cover and refrigerate (for no longer than 24 hours).

02

PASTRY CREAM

MAKES 1 LB 8 OZ (ABOUT 3½ CUPS) • PREPARATION: 10 MINUTES • COOKING: 10 MINUTES

2 cups milk
6 egg yolks
½ cup sugar
½ cup self-rising flour

OPTIONAL FLAVORINGS:
1½ oz praline, or
3 small teaspoons coffee extract, or
4½ oz chocolate, melted

1	Bring the milk to a boil in a pan. Meanwhile, beat the egg yolks with the sugar until thick and creamy. Incorporate the flour.	2	Pour half the hot milk onto the eggs, beating constantly. Return to the pan, still beating (scrape the base of the pan to stop it sticking).
3	Continue to beat and let boil for up to 2 minutes to achieve the required consistency: the more the cream boils, the thicker it will be.	4	Transfer the custard into a bowl and stir in your choice of flavoring. Cover with plastic wrap, placing it directly on the surface, let cool completely, then put in the fridge.

03

BUTTER CREAM

MAKES 10 OZ (ABOUT 1¼ CUPS) • PREPARATION: 20 MINUTES • COOKING: 5 MINUTES

½ cup butter
1 whole egg + 1 egg yolk
2 tablespoons water

scant ½ cup sugar
½ teaspoon vanilla extract (or use half vanilla extract and half coffee extract)

IN ADVANCE:
Soften the butter to a pomade then beat it for 2–3 seconds. Beat together the egg and the egg yolk in a bowl with a pouring lip.

03

1

2

3

4

5

6

1	Put the water then the sugar into a pan.	2	Cook to the "ball" stage, then pour the sugar onto the eggs.	3	Beat with an electric beater until the mixture is chilled and has trebled in volume.
4	Pour the mixture in a stream over the softened butter while continuing to beat.	5	Add the vanilla extract, or vanilla and coffee extract, and beat again.	6	Use immediately.

04

ALMOND CREAM

MAKES 10 OZ (ABOUT 1 CUP) • PREPARATION: 15 MINUTES

⅓ cup butter, softened
scant ½ cup ground almonds
⅔ cup confectioners' sugar
1 egg
1 teaspoon cornstarch
1 teaspoon rum

1 2
3 4

1	Use a wooden spoon to work the butter until completely smooth in a medium bowl.	2	Sift the ground almonds and confectioners' sugar over the butter.
3	Mix with the wooden spoon until the mixture resembles wet sand, with a few pieces of butter remaining. Add the egg and mix well.	4	When the cream is homogenous, incorporate the cornstarch and the rum. Cover with plastic wrap and store in the fridge.

05

LEMON CURD

MAKES 10 OZ (ABOUT 1½ CUPS) • PREPARATION: 15 MINUTES • COOKING: 5–10 MINUTES

4 egg yolks, carefully separated to remove all trace of whites
5 tablespoons lemon juice (1–2 lemons)

½ cup sugar
peel of ½ lemon
scant ⅓ cup butter

STORAGE:
Once completely cold, the lemon curd can be stored in a sealed jar. It will keep for 2 weeks in the fridge.

1 2

3 4

1	Beat the egg yolks in a small bowl then pour into a pan through a fine strainer.	2	Stir in the lemon juice and sugar. Put the pan over a medium heat. Stir with a flexible spatula for 5–10 minutes, scraping the sides of the pan.
3	Run your finger down the curd on the spatula: you should see a clear trace if it is cooked. The curd will continue to thicken as it cools.	4	Remove from the heat, then stir in the lemon peel and the butter, cut into cubes. Pour into a bowl and let cool.

06

CHOCOLATE MOUSSE

→ **MAKES 10 OZ (ABOUT 4 CUPS)** • PREPARATION: 20 MINUTES • COOKING: 5 MINUTES • REFRIGERATION: 2 HOURS

4 oz dark chocolate
(minimum 70% cocoa solids)
4 tablespoons butter

2 egg yolks
3 egg whites
scant ⅛ cup superfine sugar

IN ADVANCE:
Cut the chocolate and the butter into small pieces. If the eggs are cold, plunge them for a few minutes into a bowl of hot water.

1	Put the chocolate in a small pan and leave to melt over a very low heat.	2	Incorporate the butter using a whisk. Remove from the heat.	3	Add the egg yolks, one at a time, beating between each addition. Let cool.
4	Whip the egg whites until they are supple, adding the sugar midway through.	5	Fold in a quarter of the whites into the chocolate, then fold in the remaining whites until just incorporated.	6	Divide the mousse between individual ramekins. Refrigerate for at least 2 hours.

CHOCOLATE GANACHE

MAKES 3½ OZ (ABOUT ½ CUP) • PREPARATION: 5 MINUTES • COOKING: 10 MINUTES

2 oz dark chocolate
(minimum 52% cocoa solids)
1 tablespoon light cream
¼ cup milk

IN ADVANCE:
Break the chocolate into pieces.

1 2

3 4

1	Put the cream and the milk in a small pan and bring to a boil.	2	Remove from the heat and add the chocolate. Stir until it melts.
3	Return to a medium heat and cook for 2 minutes after it bubbles, stirring all the time with a flexible spatula.	4	Use immediately or pour into a bowl and cover with plastic wrap placed directly in contact with the ganache. Let cool in the fridge.

08

PANNA COTTA

MAKES 4 • PREPARATION: 15 MINUTES • COOKING: 7 MINUTES • REFRIGERATION: AT LEAST 2 HOURS

2 leaves of gelatin (¼ oz)
1 vanilla bean
1¾ cups light cream
⅓ cup sugar

IN ADVANCE:
Soften the gelatin in cold water.

Break the vanilla bean and place in a pan with the cream.

1	Heat the cream with the vanilla bean in a small pan over a medium heat.	2	When the cream starts to steam, add the sugar and beat to dissolve it.	3	Increase the heat. Once the cream simmers, remove the pan from the heat.
4	Leave for 1 minute, remove the vanilla bean, and add the gelatin (squeezed first between your fingers).	5	Beat the cream vigorously to ensure the gelatin is thoroughly incorporated.	6	Let cool for around 5 minutes, beating once or twice to prevent a skin forming. ➢

7	Carefully pour into 4 ramekins or small molds, beating frequently to ensure the vanilla seeds are evenly distributed. When the creams have cooled to room temperature, cover them with plastic wrap and place in the fridge for at least 2 hours.	**IS IT SET?** Remove one panna cotta from the fridge and gently shake it; the cream is set if it does not quiver when you shake the mold. You can turn it out or return it to the fridge until you are ready to serve.

8	To turn out the panna cotta, fill a heat-resistant bowl with boiling water. Remove the plastic wrap from the ramekins. Dip each one into the water (not quite to the top) and wait for 8–10 seconds before removing. Quickly invert onto a plate. Gently shake the dish until the panna cotta is released.	**NOTE** If you use molds that are less thick than ramekins, the heat of the water will warm them more quickly, so dip them for only 3–5 seconds before inverting onto plates.

09

CARAMEL

MAKES 3½ OZ (ABOUT ½ CUP) • PREPARATION: 5 MINUTES • COOKING: 5 MINUTES

2 tablespoons water
scant ½ cup sugar

EQUIPMENT:
Have a pastry brush handy to wet the sides of the pan with water: it helps to remove the sugar crystals.

TIP:
To clean the pan, fill it with water and bring to a boil. Beat to remove the caramel then tip everything away.

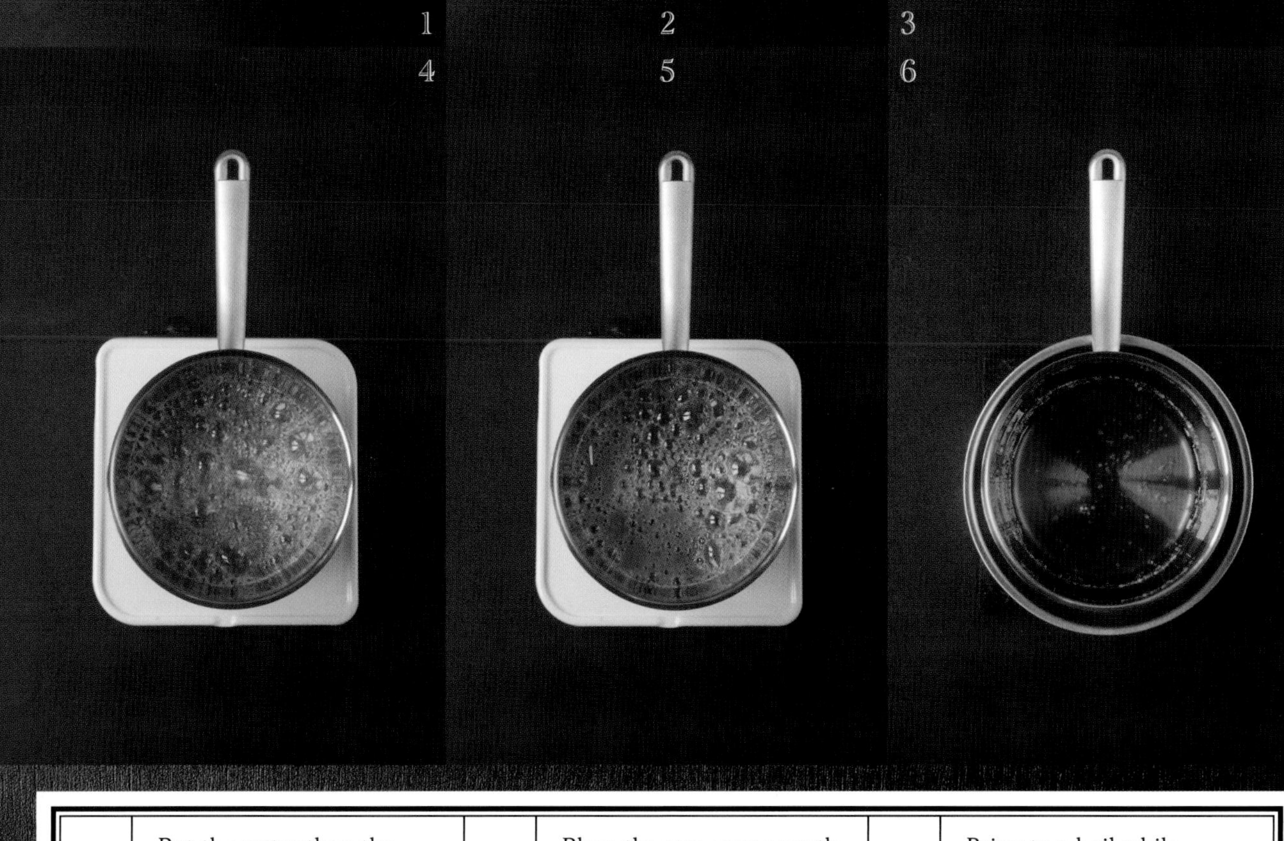

1	Put the water then the sugar into a small, heavy-based pan.	2	Place the pan over a gentle heat and beat until the sugar dissolves.	3	Bring to a boil while wetting the sides with the pastry brush dipped in water.
4	As soon as it reaches boiling point, stop stirring immediately and let the caramel color.	5	Plunge the base of the pan into cold water for a few seconds to stop the caramel from cooking.	6	Use as quickly as possible; the caramel will harden as it cools, making it difficult to work with.

SALTY BUTTER CARAMEL SAUCE

MAKES 7 OZ (ABOUT 1 CUP) • PREPARATION: 5 MINUTES • COOKING: 10 MINUTES

1 tablespoon salted butter
scant ½ cup light cream
2 tablespoons water
scant ½ cup sugar

IN ADVANCE:
Cut the butter into small pieces.

1	Heat the cream in a small pan over a medium heat.	2	Put the water then the sugar into a second small, heavy-based, pan.	3	Beat over a gentle heat until the sugar dissolves.
4	Bring to a boil. Stop stirring immediately and let the caramel take on a rich mahogany color.	5	Add all the hot cream. Mix with the whisk and leave over the heat for 2 minutes.	6	Remove from the heat and add the butter. Mix and let cool (the caramel will thicken on cooling).

CHOCOLATE SAUCE

MAKES 10 OZ (ABOUT 1½ CUPS) • PREPARATION: 5 MINUTES • COOKING: 5 MINUTES

3½ oz dark chocolate
⅜ cup milk
scant ½ cup light or whipping cream

IN ADVANCE:
Break the chocolate into pieces.

1 2

3 4

1	Bring the milk and cream to a boil in a small pan.	2	Remove from the heat and add the chocolate.
3	Mix with a flexible spatula until the chocolate is completely melted.	4	Return to the heat. Remove as soon as it starts to simmer. Use quickly.

12

RED BERRY COULIS

MAKES 7 OZ (ABOUT 1 CUP) • DEFROSTING: 10 MINUTES • PREPARATION: 5 MINUTES • COOKING: 1 MINUTE

1½ cups frozen mixed red berries
¼ cup sugar
pinch of salt
½ teaspoon lemon juice

IN ADVANCE:
Put the frozen fruit in a heat-resistant bowl and place over a pan of boiling water. Cover the bowl with plastic wrap and leave to defrost for about 10 minutes, stirring after 5 minutes.

12

1 2

3 4

1	Sprinkle the sugar and salt over the defrosted fruit while still in the water bath and mix for about 1 minute to dissolve the sugar and salt.	2	Transfer everything into the bowl of a food mixer fitted with a blade and mix for about 20 seconds until the mixture is blended evenly.
3	Rub through a fine-mesh strainer using a flexible spatula to crush the purée and extract all the juice.	4	Add the lemon juice. Mix well, cover, and put in the fridge for at least 1 hour. This coulis will keep for 4 days in the fridge.

RED BERRY COMPOTE

MAKES 8 OZ (ABOUT 2 CUPS) • DEFROSTING: 10 MINUTES • PREPARATION: 10 MINUTES • COOKING: 5 MINUTES

1½ cups frozen mixed red fruits
2 tablespoons sugar
½ teaspoon honey
2 teaspoons balsamic vinegar

IN ADVANCE:
Put the frozen fruit in a heat-resistant bowl and place over a pan of boiling water. Cover the bowl with plastic wrap and leave to defrost for about 10 minutes, stirring after 5 minutes.

1 2

3 4

1	Drain the fruit, reserving the juice. Mix 3 tablespoons of juice with the sugar, honey, and vinegar in a pan. Place over a medium heat to dissolve the sugar, beating occasionally.	2	Bring to a boil to thicken it. To check it is cooked, dip a small spoon into the pan and bring it out again; the syrup should coat the back of the spoon.
3	Let cool before adding the drained fruit. The syrup will thicken further on cooling.	4	Mix together. When the compote is cold, cover with plastic wrap and place in the fridge.

CHANTILLY CREAM

MAKES 1 LB 2 OZ • PREPARATION: 10 MINUTES

½ cup confectioners' sugar
1 vanilla bean
2¼ cups whipping cream, chilled (or use one-third heavy cream to two-thirds milk)

IN ADVANCE:
Fill a bowl larger than your mixing bowl with ice cubes and very cold water.

TIP:
To make a small quantity of Chantilly cream, use a bowl with high sides and dispense with the iced water bath.

1	Put the confectioners' sugar in a medium bowl and add the vanilla seeds scraped from the bean.	2	Plunge the base of the bowl in the prepared iced water and pour in the chilled cream.
3	Tilt the bowl to maximize the amount of air and beat using an electric beater on its highest setting.		**CHANTILLY IN A SIPHON** Pour the cream, sugar, and vanilla seeds into a cream siphon. Close and attach the gas capsule according to manufacturer's instructions. Shake vigorously.

15

PLAIN FROSTING

MAKES 3½ OZ (ABOUT ½ CUP) • PREPARATION: 5 MINUTES

½ egg white
⅞ cup confectioners' sugar
1 teaspoon lemon juice

FOR A THICKER FROSTING:
Add up to ¼ cup extra confectioners' sugar.

STORAGE:
This keeps for several days in the fridge or for a month in the freezer if sealed. After refrigeration, work the frosting again with a little confectioners' sugar.

1 2
3 4

1	Put the egg white in a bowl and add the confectioners' sugar.	2	Mix with a wooden spatula for 2 minutes until you have a white cream.
3	Add the lemon juice at the end and beat for 10 seconds.	4	Trickle the frosting over your cake, spreading it with a palette knife. Leave for a few minutes for the frosting to set before serving.

16

CHOCOLATE FROSTING

MAKES 7 OZ (ABOUT 1 CUP) • PREPARATION: 5 MINUTES • COOKING: 10 MINUTES

3½ oz dark chocolate
3 tablespoons butter
3 tablespoons water
⅝ cup confectioners' sugar

IN ADVANCE:
Break the chocolate into pieces and cut up the butter.

1	Put the chocolate into a small pan and let melt over a very low heat (or use a double boiler), stirring with a flexible spatula until smooth.	2	Still over the heat, add the butter and the confectioners' sugar. Leave to melt, mixing everything together.
3	Remove from the heat and add the water, a spoonful at a time. If the mixture isn't smooth, put back over the heat and stir again. Let cool (not too much, or it won't spread easily).	4	Spread in a fairly thick layer over the cake using a palette knife. Take care not to leave any fingerprints, because this frosting does not set completely.

SIMPLE CAKES

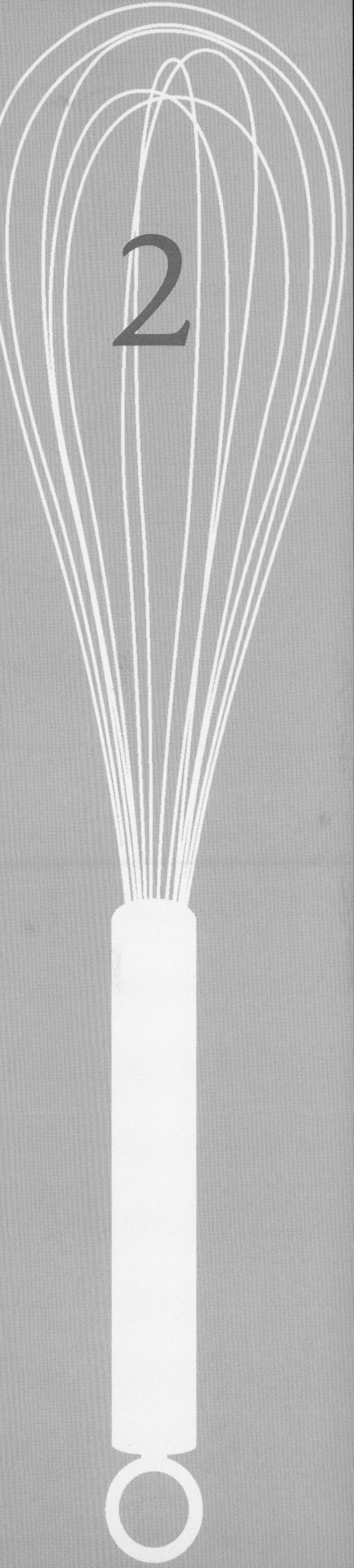

CLASSIC CAKES

Yogurt cake 17
Butter cake 18
Marbled cake 19

CHOCOLATE CAKES

Chocolate fondants 20
Flour-free chocolate cake 21
Brownies 22
Chocolate truffle cake 23

MADE IN THE U.S.

Carrot cake 24
Banana & walnut bread 25
Gingerbread 26
Corn bread 27

YOGURT CAKE

SERVES 8 • PREPARATION: 15 MINUTES • COOKING: 50 MINUTES

3 eggs
4 fl oz (1 yogurt pot) natural yogurt
4 fl oz (1 yogurt pot) sunflower or other unscented oil + extra for greasing
8 oz (2 yogurt pots) sugar
2 tablespoons lemon juice
8 oz (3 yogurt pots) all-purpose flour
1 teaspoon (½ sachet) baking powder
pinch of salt

IN ADVANCE:
Preheat the oven to 350°F. Lightly oil a 9-inch nonstick cake pan.

1	Break the eggs into a large bowl and beat well.	2	Beat in the yogurt.	3	Pour in the oil and beat again to combine.
4	Add in the sugar, continuing to beat, then finally the lemon juice.	5	Sift together the flour, baking powder, and salt. Add to the liquid mixture and beat again.	6	Pour the batter into the prepared cake pan and cook for 50 minutes. Turn out onto a wire rack to cool.

BUTTER CAKE

SERVES 8–10 • PREPARATION: 25 MINUTES • COOKING: 50 MINUTES

1 cup softened butter + extra for greasing
1⅓ cups sugar
3 eggs + 3 egg yolks
1 teaspoon vanilla extract
1½ teaspoons water
1 teaspoon salt
1¾ cups self-rising flour

IN ADVANCE:
Preheat the oven to 325°F and put a rack in the center of the oven. Thoroughly grease a savarin mold and place in the fridge.

1 2

3 4

1	Use an electric beater to beat the butter until really smooth (about 15 seconds).	2	Keep beating while slowly sprinkling the sugar over the butter (this should take about 30 seconds). Beat for 4–5 minutes until the butter is almost white.	
3	Mix the eggs and the yolks with the vanilla extract and the water in a bowl with a pouring lip.	4	Very slowly pour the egg mixture over the butter while beating at medium speed. Add the salt and beat again.	➢

18

5

Add in one-third of the flour and incorporate with a flexible spatula then add in the remaining flour, in two further thirds, making sure the flour is incorporated before adding in the final third.

Pour the batter into the prepared pan and smooth the surface with the back of a spoon. Bake for 50 minutes.

6	Leave in the pan for 5 minutes before turning out the cake onto a plate, then let cool on a wire rack.	**TIP** ☛ To ensure the batter is even in texture, use eggs at room temperature. If you keep your eggs in the fridge, plunge them into a bowl of hot water for several minutes before using. Don't despair if your batter looks curdled (as shown in photo 5), the final result will be unaffected!

19

MARBLED CAKE

SERVES 8 • PREPARATION: 30 MINUTES • COOKING: 1 HOUR 5 MINUTES

$\frac{7}{8}$ cup butter + extra for greasing
4 eggs
$\frac{7}{8}$ cup sugar
1 teaspoon salt

scant 2 cups self-rising flour
1 tablespoon or 2 sachets vanilla sugar
$\frac{1}{4}$ cup unsweetened cocoa powder

IN ADVANCE:
Preheat the oven to 350°F and put a rack in the center of the oven. Grease an 11-inch loaf pan.

1	Melt the butter in a small pan then remove it immediately from the heat.	2	Separate the eggs into two large bowls.	
3	Add the sugar and the salt to the egg yolks. Mix thoroughly with a wooden spoon.	4	Add alternately small amounts of flour and melted butter to the eggs, beating between each addition.	➢

19

5 6

7 8

5	Whip the egg whites into a meringue, adding half the vanilla sugar midway through.	6	Use a wooden spoon to incorporate the meringue into the batter.
7	Divide the batter between two bowls. Add the cocoa powder to one bowl and the remaining vanilla sugar to the other.	8	Using a dessertspoon, spoon the two batters alternately into the loaf pan to create a marbled effect.

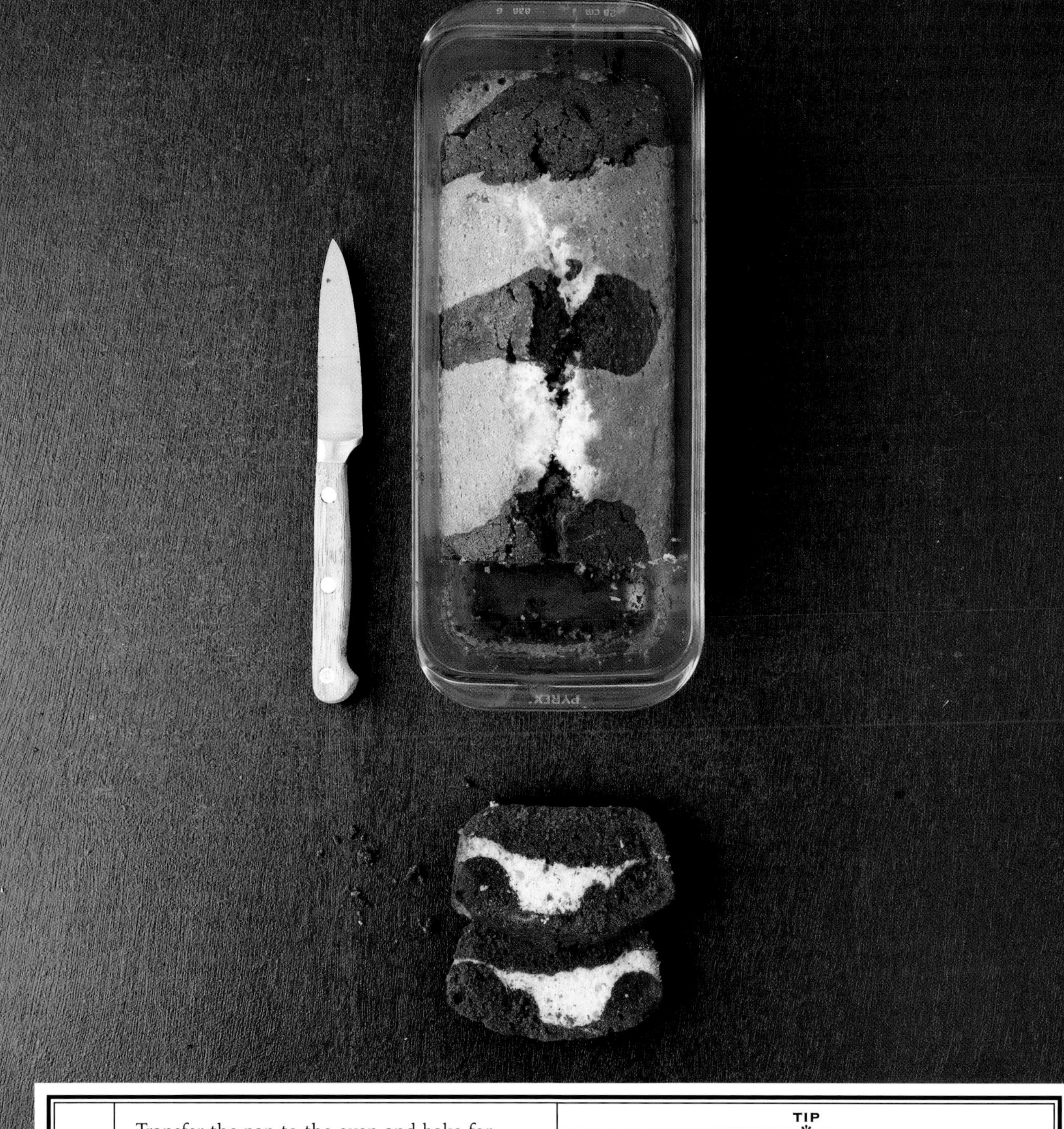

9 Transfer the pan to the oven and bake for 1 hour. Put the tip of a sharp knife into the center of the cake to check it is cooked; the knife should come out clean.

TIP

In most recipes that call for whipped egg whites, the whites have to be delicately folded into the batter, otherwise they break down. For this recipe, though, you don't have to be so careful when you add the whites because the final texture of this cake is more dense.

CHOCOLATE FONDANTS

SERVES 4 • PREPARATION: 15 MINUTES • COOKING: 15–18 MINUTES

½ cup butter
3½ oz chocolate
4 eggs

½ cup sugar
½ cup self-rising flour

IN ADVANCE:
Preheat the oven to 350°F and put a rack in the center of the oven.

1	Cut the butter into pieces and put into a small pan. Break the chocolate into pieces and place on top of the butter.	2	Put the pan over a low heat and stir with a flexible spatula as soon as the butter starts to melt.
3	Keep stirring until the chocolate and butter are smooth and combined, then remove from the heat.	4	Break the eggs into a bowl with a pouring lip and beat with the sugar until smooth (about 10 seconds). ➢

5

6 7

5 Pour the melted chocolate–butter mixture over the eggs and mix as lightly as possible with a whisk.

6 Add the flour in three lots, mixing with a flexible spatula between each addition.

7 Use the batter to fill 4 ramekins or molds 3½ inches in diameter with sides 2 inches tall. Transfer to the oven for 15–18 minutes.

IS IT COOKED?	TIP
Shake one ramekin while still in the oven; the center should barely wobble. Note that the cooking time will depend on the size and thickness of your dishes.	☛ You can prepare this dessert in advance. Cover each filled ramekin or mold with plastic wrap and place in the fridge until you are ready to cook. Remove the plastic wrap and cook them straight from the fridge for 17–20 minutes.

21

FLOUR-FREE CHOCOLATE CAKE

MAKES 8 • PREPARATION: 20 MINUTES • COOKING: 25 MINUTES

5 eggs
¾ cup sugar
¾ cup butter + extra for greasing

7 oz dark chocolate (minimum 70% cocoa solids)
scant ½ cup ground almonds, sifted

IN ADVANCE:
Preheat the oven to 350°F and put a rack in the center of the oven. Grease a 9-inch square cake pan and place in the fridge.

1	Beat the eggs in a large bowl, just enough to break the yolks, then add the sugar. Combine the mixture with a whisk, stopping as soon as it is evenly blended.	2	Put the butter and the chocolate in a pan over a medium heat. When the butter has melted, turn off the heat and stir with a flexible spatula until the chocolate has also melted.
3	Pour the chocolate over the eggs and very lightly mix with the whisk. Add the ground almonds and mix again.	4	Pour the batter into the pan, and give it a tap on the counter top to release any air bubbles. Transfer to the oven for 25 minutes maximum.

BROWNIES

SERVES 8–10 • PREPARATION: 20 MINUTES • RESTING: 10 MINUTES • COOKING: 35 MINUTES

1 cup walnuts
⅞ cup butter + extra for greasing
4 oz dark chocolate (minimum 70% cocoa solids)
1 cup sugar
4 eggs
¼ teaspoon vanilla extract
1½ cups self-rising flour
pinch of salt

IN ADVANCE:
Preheat the oven to 350°F and put a rack in the center of the oven. Grease a 9-inch square cake pan. Cut the butter and break the chocolate into pieces.

1	Roughly chop the walnuts with a knife or break them with your fingers.	2	Put the butter in a pan then put the chocolate on top.	3	Place over a gentle heat and stir with a flexible spatula until the butter melts.	
4	Add the sugar and mix for 2 minutes (the sugar will not completely dissolve). Remove from the heat.	5	Pour the batter into a bowl, leave for 10 minutes to cool, then add the eggs, one at a time, beating well.	6	Add the vanilla extract and beat again to combine.	➢

7 8

9 10

7	Sift together the flour and the salt into a separate bowl. Tip it onto the melted chocolate.	8	Work in the flour with a flexible spatula until it is completely incorporated.
9	Lastly, add the walnuts and mix again.	10	Pour the batter into the prepared pan. Transfer to the oven for 20–25 minutes. When it is cooked, let cool on a wire rack.

IS IT COOKED?	STORAGE
When cooked, the brownie should not move if you shake the pan but the blade of a knife inserted into the center will not come out clean.	Cut the brownies into 2½-inch squares. You can wrap them individually in plastic wrap if you don't want to eat them immediately. This way, they will keep up to 4 days in the fridge.

23

CHOCOLATE TRUFFLE CAKE

SERVES 6 • PREPARATION: 15 MINUTES • COOKING: 35 MINUTES

3 eggs
⅔ cup sugar
⅔ cup water
7 oz dark chocolate
(minimum 52% cocoa solids)

⅝ cup butter
¼ cup all-purpose flour
unsweetened cocoa powder, for dusting

IN ADVANCE:
Preheat the oven to 350°F and put a rack in the center of the oven (see page 71). Butter a 9-inch cake pan and line the base with parchment paper.

1	Break the eggs into a bowl, beat well, and set aside.	2	Put the sugar and water in a pan, place over a medium heat, and beat to dissolve the sugar.	3	When the sugar has dissolved, bring to a boil then remove immediately from the heat.	
4	Add the chocolate in pieces and mix until it has melted.	5	Next add the butter, in cubes, and mix until it is fully incorporated.	6	After 5 minutes, add the beaten eggs.	➢

23

7 8
9 10

7	Sprinkle the flour over the chocolate mixture and incorporate it with the whisk.	8	Pour the batter into the prepared pan and transfer to the oven. Cook the cake for 30 minutes or until the center no longer wobbles.
9	Remove the cake and let cool on a wire rack for 5 minutes before turning out onto a plate.	10	When the cake is complete cold, cover in plastic wrap.

11	Put the cake into the fridge until you are ready to serve (it is best served chilled). To decorate, dust with unsweetened cocoa powder just before serving.

COOKING IN THE OVEN WITH A WATER BATH

☛ When you preheat the oven, put in a second rack under the first. Place a shallow ovenproof dish on this rack and, just before putting the cake into the oven, fill the dish with hot water.

CARROT CAKE

SERVES 8 • PREPARATION: 20 MINUTES • COOKING: 55 MINUTES

1½ cups all-purpose flour + 1 teaspoon salt
1 teaspoon each of baking powder, baking soda, powdered cinnamon, mixed spice
3 eggs
⅞ cup sugar
⅞ cup sunflower oil
¼ cup apple purée
3 cups, lightly packed, shredded carrots
½ cup walnuts, roughly chopped
½ cup raisins

IN ADVANCE:
Preheat the oven to 350°F and put a rack in the center of the oven with a cookie sheet on it. Grease and line an 11-inch loaf pan.

1	Sift the flour, salt, baking powder, baking soda, and spices into a large bowl. Make a well in the center.	2	In a separate bowl, beat the eggs just enough to break the yolks.	3	Add the sugar and beat until thick and creamy.
4	Pour in the oil slowly in a steady stream, whisking as if making mayonnaise.	5	Next add the apple purée.	6	Pour the mixture into the well in the center of the flour. ➢

7	Stir the batter using a flexible spatula then add the shredded carrot, walnuts, and raisins. Continue to work the batter until evenly blended then transfer it to the prepared loaf pan.	**TIP** ☛ To remove any air bubbles and firm the batter in the pan, give it a tap on the counter top before putting in the oven.

8	Bake the cake for 55 minutes on the prepared cookie sheet. When it is cooked, run the blade of a knife around the sides of the pan. Let stand for 15 minutes before turning out onto a wire rack. Let cool completely before frosting (see overleaf). To serve, cut into 1-inch thick slices.	**IS IT COOKED?** ☛ When the cake is cooked it will be a dark reddish-brown. The tip of a sharp knife inserted into the center of the cake should come out completely clean.

CARROT CAKE FROSTING

MAKES ABOUT 5 OZ (3/4 CUP) • PREPARATION: 10 MINUTES

2 tablespoons butter
2 tablespoons cream cheese
½ teaspoon lemon juice
¼ teaspoon vanilla extract
½ cup confectioners' sugar

IN ADVANCE:
Cut the butter into pieces and work into a pomade.

1 2

3 4

1	Use a wooden spatula to work the butter and the cream cheese together until pale and completely smooth.	2	Transfer to the bowl of a food mixer, add the lemon juice and vanilla extract, and mix for no more than 5 seconds. Scrape the sides of the bowl with a spatula.
3	Add the confectioners' sugar and mix again for no more than 10 seconds until the mixture is creamy.	4	Cover with plastic wrap and keep for up to 4 days in the fridge. Spread over the carrot cake just before serving.

BANANA & WALNUT BREAD

SERVES 8–10 • PREPARATION: 25 MINUTES • COOKING: 50 MINUTES TO 1 HOUR

⅔ cup softened butter
⅔ cup sugar
3 eggs at room temperature
4 bananas

2 teaspoons vanilla extract
¾ cup walnuts
3 cups all-purpose flour
2 teaspoons baking powder

IN ADVANCE:
Preheat the oven to 325°F. Thoroughly grease a savarin mold or use a nonstick one.

1 2

3 4

1	Beat the butter for 15 seconds using an electric beater then add the sugar.	2	Continue to beat for several minutes until the mixture is pale, light, and fluffy.	
3	Beat the eggs well in a bowl, preferably one with a pouring lip, then pour them very slowly on the butter–sugar mixture while continuing to beat at medium speed.	4	Crush the bananas with a fork and add them to the batter, along with the vanilla extract. Work them in using a hand whisk.	➢

5	Roughly chop the walnuts and put them in a bowl. Sift in the flour and baking powder and mix together.		Incorporate the dry ingredients into the banana mixture and work everything together smoothly using a flexible spatula.

6	Pour the mixture into the savarin mold and place it on a cookie sheet. Transfer to the oven and bake for 50 minutes to 1 hour. When the cake is cooked, leave it in the pan for 15 minutes before turning out. Enjoy just as it is, cut into medium slices, or with butter and preserves.	**OPTION** You can also use a classic (11-inch) loaf pan, and bake it at 350°F. Whichever shape cake pan you use, the cooking test is the same: insert the blade of a sharp pointed knife right into the cake; it should come out clean.

GINGERBREAD

→ **SERVES 8–10** • PREPARATION: 14 MINUTES • COOKING: 1 HOUR ←

3 cups all-purpose flour and a pinch of salt
1 teaspoon each of baking soda, powdered ginger, allspice
½ teaspoon each powdered cinnamon, powdered nutmeg, unsweetened cocoa powder

½ cup butter + extra for greasing
1 scant cup maple syrup
⅔ cup sugar
½ cup cultured buttermilk
½ cup milk and 1 egg

IN ADVANCE:
Preheat the oven to 350°F.
Ensure the liquid ingredients and the egg are all at room temperature. Melt the butter.

1	Mix the flour, salt, baking soda, spices, and unsweetened cocoa powder in a medium bowl.	2	Put the melted butter, maple syrup, sugar, buttermilk, milk, and the egg in a separate, large bowl.	
3	Thoroughly mix the liquid ingredients using an electric beater on slow speed.	4	Add the dry ingredients and beat on medium speed until the batter is smooth and evenly blended.	➢

5

Thoroughly grease an 11-inch loaf pan or mold. Pour the batter into the pan, transfer to the oven, and bake for 55 minutes.

TIP

☛ To make sure the cake doesn't burn, stand the pan on a cookie sheet.

		TO SERVE
6	Remove the cake from the oven and let cool for 10 minutes before turning out onto a wire rack. Once it has cooled to room temperature, cover in plastic wrap.	Enjoy warm or at room temperature, as it is or with a little sour cream or heavy cream. This cake will keep for up to 5 days if covered in plastic wrap and stored at room temperature.

27

CORN BREAD

SERVES 8 • PREPARATION: 15 MINUTES • COOKING: 30 MINUTES

2 tablespoons melted butter + extra for greasing
1 cup cornmeal, see page 89
1⅓ cups plain flour
2 teaspoons baking powder
1 teaspoon baking soda
2 tablespoons sugar + 1 teaspoon salt
2 eggs
⅝ cup milk
⅝ cup cultured buttermilk

IN ADVANCE:
Preheat the oven to 425°F and put a rack in the center of the oven. Grease an 11-inch loaf pan or a 7-inch square cake pan.

1 2

3 4

1	Melt the butter in a small saucepan. Remove immediately from the heat.	2	Put the polenta, flour, baking powder, baking soda, sugar, and salt in a large bowl.	
3	Mix all the dry ingredients together and make a well in the center.	4	Break the eggs into the well and mix in gently using a wooden spoon.	➢

5 6

7 8

5	Add the milk and buttermilk. Mix well until the dry ingredients are fully incorporated.	6	Pour in the melted butter and mix again until everything is evenly blended.
7	Pour the batter into the cake pan. Transfer to the oven and cook for 30 minutes.	8	When the top is golden brown, remove the cake from the oven and turn out onto a wire rack to cool for 5–10 minutes.

TO SERVE		TO REHEAT
9	Serve cut into small squares or slices. Enjoy the corn bread warm, with a knob of butter. You can eat it on its own, as a cake, or as an accompaniment to savory dishes (with soup or vegetables, for example).	Cover the bread if not serving immediately. Reheat for 5–10 minutes at 350°F. **NOTE** Many brands of cornmeal are precooked. You can use this type in the recipe, but the result will turn out a little drier.

LAYERED CAKES

CHOUX PASTRY

Choux pastry 28
Praline choux 29
Caramel glaze 30
Profiteroles 31
Chocolate eclairs 32
Choux puffs 33
Rose St-Honoré choux 34

PUFF PASTRY

Puff pastry 35
Mille-feuilles 36
Kings' cake 37

CHEESECAKES

Tiramisu 38
Mascarpone cheesecake 39
Corsican cheesecake 40

FILLED CAKES

Jelly roll 41
Coffee log 42
Poppyseed cake 43
Chocolate charlotte 44
Vacherin 45

CHOUX PASTRY

→ **MAKES 10 OZ** • PREPARATION: 20 MINUTES • COOKING: 15–20 MINUTES ←

2 eggs
8 tablespoons water
½ cup butter, cut into small dice
½ teaspoon salt
⅝ cup self-rising flour

IN ADVANCE:
Preheat the oven to 425°F and put a rack in the center of the oven. Line a cookie sheet with parchment paper. Break the eggs into a bowl, beat well, and set aside.

1	Put the water, butter, and salt in a pan over a medium heat just long enough to melt the butter.	2	Bring to a rolling boil. Immediately remove from the heat and place on a panstand. Add the flour in one go.	
3	Mix with a wooden spoon until it leaves the sides of the pan and makes a ball of dough.	4	Stir in half the beaten eggs and incorporate thoroughly before adding the rest.	➢

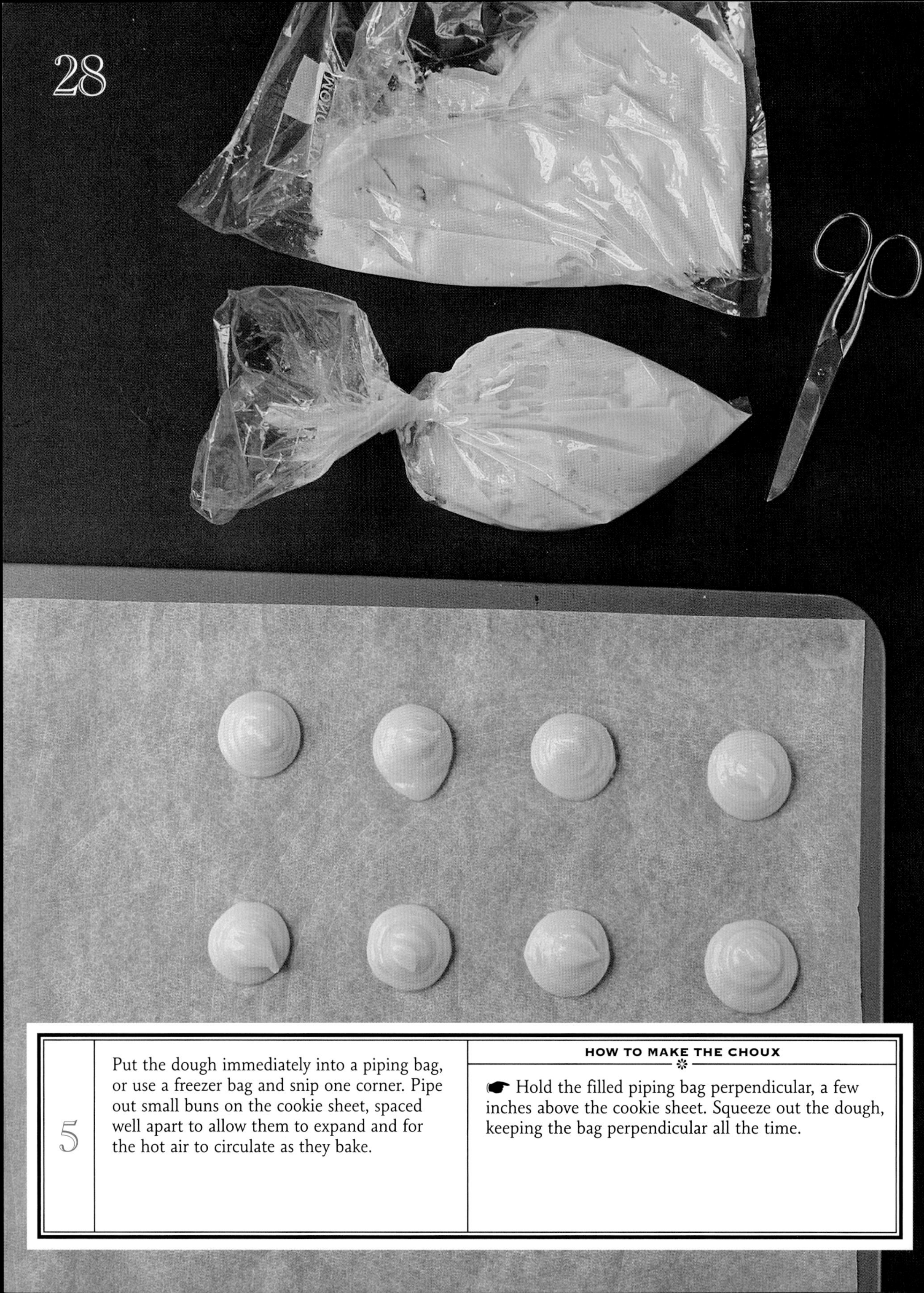

5	Put the dough immediately into a piping bag, or use a freezer bag and snip one corner. Pipe out small buns on the cookie sheet, spaced well apart to allow them to expand and for the hot air to circulate as they bake.	**HOW TO MAKE THE CHOUX** ☛ Hold the filled piping bag perpendicular, a few inches above the cookie sheet. Squeeze out the dough, keeping the bag perpendicular all the time.

6	Transfer the buns to the oven and bake for 10 minutes, then wedge open the oven door with a wooden spoon and bake for a further 5 minutes. Let cool on a wire rack.	**FOR LIGHT AND PUFFY CHOUX** Just before putting the sheet in the oven, prick the buns lightly with the wetted tines of a fork. This gives them an even shape and helps them to puff up as they cook. Wait until the buns are lightly colored before opening the oven door.

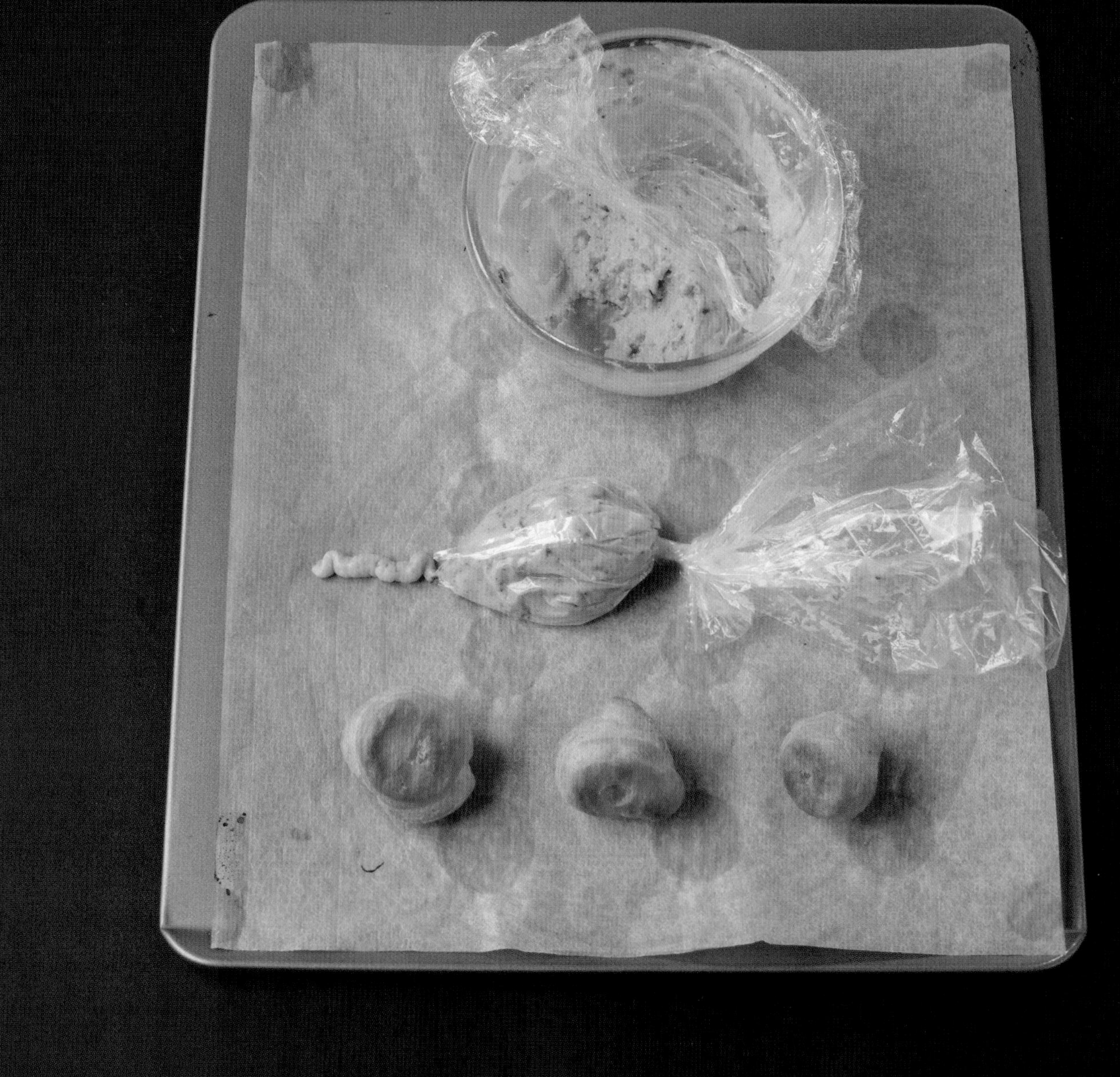

PRALINE CHOUX

ENOUGH FOR 20–25 CHOUX

Prepare 1 lb 8 oz praline-flavored Pastry Cream (see recipe 02) and 25 choux (see recipe 28).

Fill a piping bag with the prepared cream. Pierce the base of each bun with the tip of a sharp knife and insert the nozzle. Squeeze the bag to fill each bun with cream. Place the filled buns upright again.

CARAMEL GLAZE

ENOUGH FOR 25 CHOUX

Once you have filled the choux buns, prepare about ½ cup of Caramel (see recipe 09).

Stop the cooking before it darkens too much (the caramel will continue to color off the heat).

Immediately dip the top of each bun into the caramel then place them on a cooling rack.

31

PROFITEROLES

✤ MAKES 20 • PREPARATION: 10 MINUTES • COOKING: 5 MINUTES ✤

20 choux made with 10 oz Choux Pastry (see recipe 28)
17 fl oz vanilla ice cream

CHOCOLATE SAUCE:
3½ oz chocolate
6 tablespoons milk
6 tablespoons light cream

IN ADVANCE:
Let the choux buns cool slightly then slice off the top third with a serrated knife. Take the ice cream out of the freezer. Break the chocolate into pieces.

1 2

3 4

1	To make the chocolate sauce, pour the milk and cream into a pan and bring to the boil.	2	Remove from the heat, add the chocolate, and stir until smooth. Return to the heat and let bubble gently then remove and set aside.
3	Use a teaspoon to top the sliced buns generously with the softened ice cream, allowing it to overspill a little. Replace the caps.	4	Pour a little hot chocolate sauce into the base of small serving dishes. Place 2 profiteroles in each dish and serve with extra chocolate sauce.

CHOCOLATE ECLAIRS

MAKES 20 • PREPARATION: 10 MINUTES • COOKING: 5 MINUTES

20 eclairs, 4 inches long, made with
10 oz Choux Pastry (see recipe 28)
1 lb 8 oz Pastry Cream
flavored with chocolate (see recipe 02)

CHOCOLATE FROSTING:
3½ oz dark chocolate
⅝ cup confectioners' sugar
3 tablespoons butter
3 tablespoons water

IN ADVANCE:
Slit the eclairs down one side with a serrated knife and fill them with the pastry cream using a piping bag. Cut the butter into dice.

1 2

3 4

1	To make the frosting, melt the chocolate in a pan over a very low heat (or in a water bath). Stir with a flexible spatula.	2	Keep the pan over a very low heat, add the confectioners' sugar and the butter. Let melt, stirring all the time. Remove from the heat and add the water, a spoonful at a time.
3	Let the frosting cool slightly: too hot and it will run; too cold and it will not spread so easily.	4	Place the filled eclairs on a rack and spread each one with a thickish layer of frosting using a palette knife.

CHOUX PUFFS

MAKES 25 • PREPARATION: 20 MINUTES • COOKING: 14 MINUTES

CHOUX PASTRY:
8 tablespoons water
½ cup butter, cut into dice
½ teaspoon salt
1 teaspoon sugar
⅔ cup self-rising flour
2 eggs
sugar nibs (large grain sugar), to decorate

IN ADVANCE:
Preheat the oven to 400°F.

1	Prepare the choux pastry, following the method in recipe 28, by heating the water, butter, salt, and sugar. Add the flour and eggs as described in steps 3 and 4.	Pipe out mini choux buns, spaced well apart, on a cookie sheet. Sprinkle them with the sugar nibs.	Transfer the sheet to the oven and bake for 15 minutes, then prop open the oven door with a wooden spoon and bake for a further 5 minutes. Remove the buns from the oven and let cool on the sheet.

ROSE ST-HONORÉ CHOUX

MAKES 4 • PREPARATION: 20 MINUTES • COOKING: 15–20 MINUTES

12 oz Pastry Cream (see recipe 02), flavored with ¼ teaspoon rose water
10 oz Choux Pastry (see recipe 28)

8 oz Chantilly Cream (see recipe 14), mixed with 2 drops of pink food coloring
3½ oz Plain Frosting (see recipe 15), mixed with 2 drops of pink food coloring

IN ADVANCE:
Cover a cookie sheet with parchment paper. Preheat the oven to 425°F. Prepare the pastry cream, adding the rose water with the milk.

1 3
2

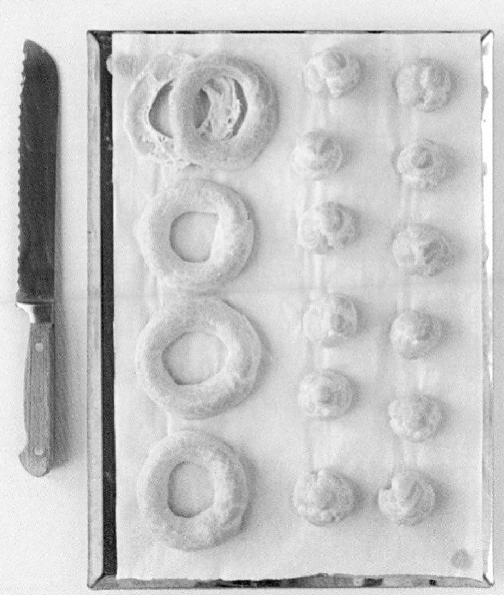

1	Pipe 4 crowns and 12 mini buns on the sheet. Cook for 10–15 minutes. Prop open the oven door with a wooden spoon, bake for 5 minutes.	3	Prepare the frosting (see recipe 15), adding in the food coloring at the end.	➢
2	Remove from the oven, leave for 10 minutes then place the choux on a wire rack. Cut each crown in two across the middle with a serrated knife, and pierce the base of the mini buns.			

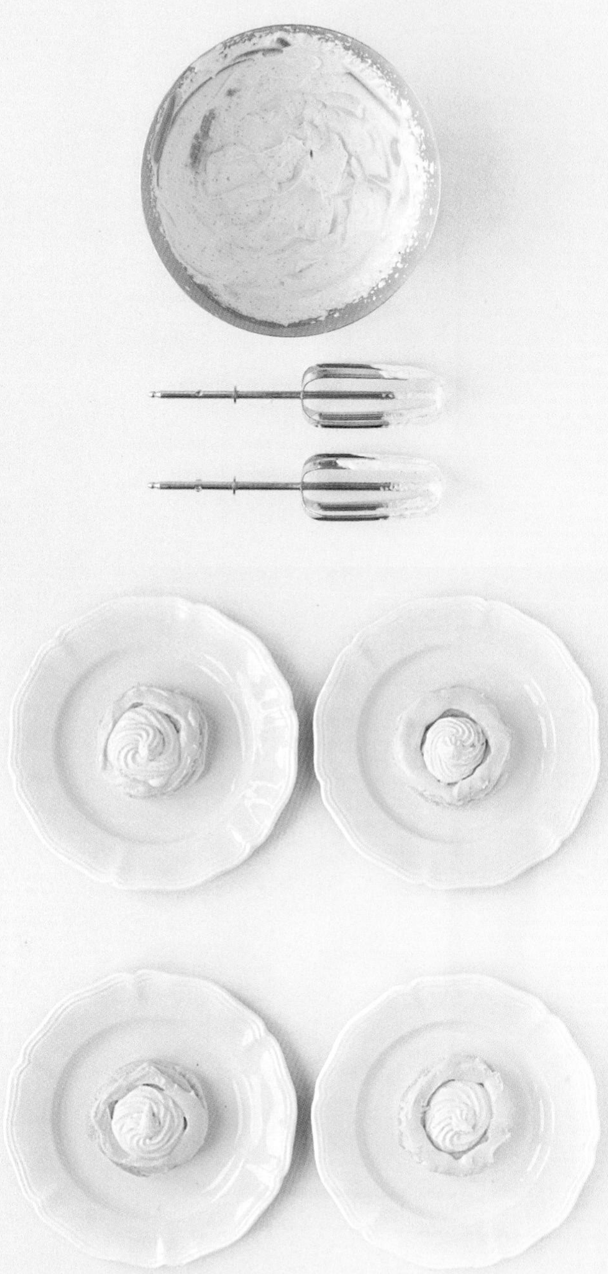

5	Using a piping bag, fill the base of the 4 crowns with pastry cream then replace the tops. Fill the bases of the mini buns, too. Ice the tops of the buns and the filled crowns using a fine-bladed spatula (or a smooth-bladed knife).	6	Prepare the Chantilly (see recipe 14), adding in the food coloring with the cream at the outset.
		7	Arrange the filled crowns on plates and top each one with Chantilly. Place the mini buns on the crowns.

8 Serve immediately (or keep in a cool place for no more than 1 hour before serving).

OPTION

For a stronger rose flavor, add ¼ teaspoon rose water to the cream before whipping the Chantilly.

TO SIMPLIFY THE TASK OF FROSTING

You can make the frosting more liquid by adding a few extra drops of lemon juice then simply dip the top of each crown and mini buns in the frosting.

PUFF PASTRY

MAKES ABOUT 1 LB 12 OZ • PREPARATION: 30 MINUTES • REFRIGERATION: 2 HOURS

3 cups all-purpose flour
$1\frac{1}{4}$ cups + 2 tablespoons butter
$\frac{5}{8}$ cup very cold water

3 teaspoons sugar
$\frac{1}{2}$ teaspoon salt

IN ADVANCE:
Sift the flour onto a pastry board and place the butter, diced, on top.

1

2

3

4

5

6

1	Rub the butter into the flour until it forms crumbs. Make a well in the center and add the water.	2	Add the sugar and salt and dissolve in the water using your fingertips. Work in the crumb mixture.	3	You will have a lumpy batter in the middle. Bring all the crumb mixture into this batter.	
4	When the dough forms, press down bit by bit using the palm of your hand.	5	Bring to a whole, press down once and make it into a ball.	6	Shape as a block, cover in plastic wrap, and refrigerate for 1 hour.	➢

7 8 9

10 11 12

7	Remove the pastry from the fridge and place on a lightly floured pastry board. Put a rolling pin on the pastry.	8	Roll out to form a rectangle measuring approximately 16 x 10 inches.	9	Fold a third of the pastry along its long side into the center then fold the other long side on top.
10	Do the same with the short side, folding the pastry in on itself.	11	Lightly press down using the palm of your hand.	12	Roll out again to form a rectangle measuring about 16 x 10 inches.

13 14
15 16

13	Repeat these steps: flour the pastry board and roll out the pastry a third time to make a rectangle measuring 16 x 10 inches.	14	Once again fold the pastry into three as in step 9.
15	Now fold into three on the short side as in step 10.	16	If you only need half the pastry, flatten it into a rectangle measuring 8 x 4 inches and cut in two (you can freeze one half). Refrigerate the pastry for 1 hour before use.

MILLE-FEUILLES

→ MAKES 4 • PREPARATION: 25 MINUTES • COOKING: 15 MINUTES ←

12 oz Pastry Cream (see recipe 02)
2 oz Chantilly Cream (see recipe 14)
14½ oz Puff Pastry (see recipe 35)
⅛ cup confectioners' sugar

IN ADVANCE:
Prepare the pastry cream, not too thick, and put in the fridge to chill.

Preheat the oven to 425°F.
Line a cookie sheet with parchment paper.

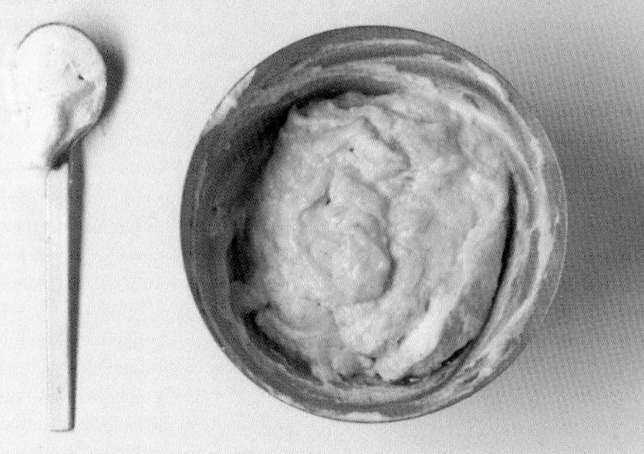

1 2
3 4

1	Remove the chilled pastry cream from the fridge and incorporate the Chantilly, a spoonful at a time.	2	Cover the bowl with plastic wrap and return to the fridge.	
3	Thinly roll out the pastry to a rectangle the size of your cookie sheet and about ⅛ inch thick.	4	Cut the pastry into 12 neat rectangles (trim off the edges) using a sharp knife. Prick each one with a small fork.	➢

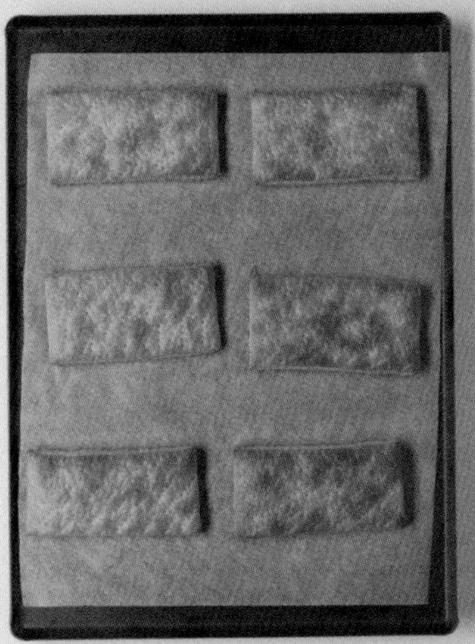

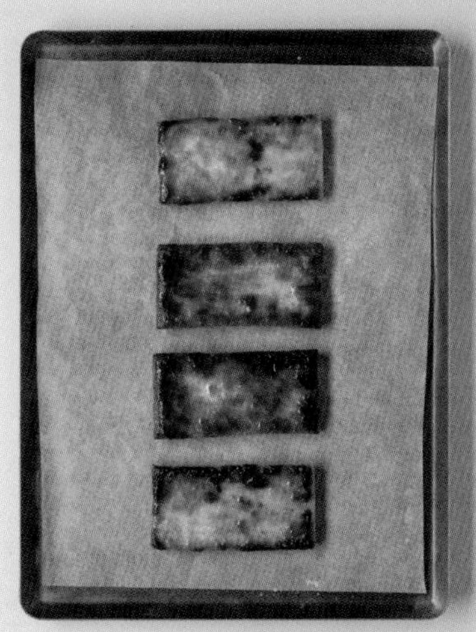

5 6

7 8

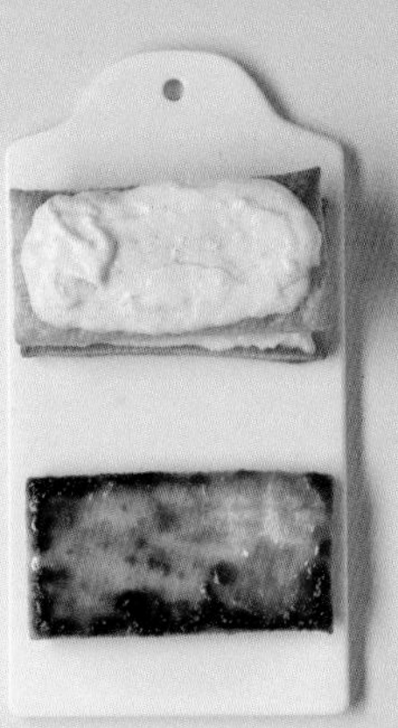

5	Place half the rectangles on the cookie sheet (and the rest in the fridge) and bake for 10 minutes (they should not be too brown). Bake the second batch in the same way.	6	Preheat the broiler. Select 4 rectangles, turn them underside (non-risen) face up, sprinkle with confectioners' sugar, and flash them under the hot broiler for 1 minute to caramelize.
7	Spread a layer of pastry cream on the remaining rectangles.	8	Build up the rectangles in pairs then top with the caramelized slice.

9	Serve the mille-feuilles as soon as possible, so that the cream doesn't have time to soak into the pastry layers.	**SERVING OPTION** You can also present this as a cake, trimming up the sides first, before cutting into slices. **VARIATION** For a very light cream filling, increase the proportion of Chantilly to pastry cream.

37

KINGS' CAKE

SERVES 6–8 • PREPARATION: 30 MINUTES • COOKING: 35 MINUTES • RESTING: 30 MINUTES

FRANGIPAN:
12 oz Pastry Cream (see recipe 02)
10 oz Almond Cream (se recipe 04)

14½ oz Puff Pastry (see recipe 35)
1 beaten egg, for glazing

IN ADVANCE:
Preheat the oven to 475°F. Make the pastry cream, not too thick, and weigh out 4 oz for this recipe. Keep the remainder in the fridge.

1	For the frangipan, mix the pastry cream into the almond cream, a spoonful at a time. Cover with plastic wrap and refrigerate.	2	Remove the pastry from the fridge. Cut in two and roll out each half to make two large squares measuring about 10 inches.
3	Place one square on a cookie sheet covered with parchment paper. Using a cake pan to guide you, cut out a 9-inch circle.	4	Make a ½ inch wash of beaten egg around the edge of the circle. Cut out a second circle from the remaining square of pastry on the pastry board. ➢

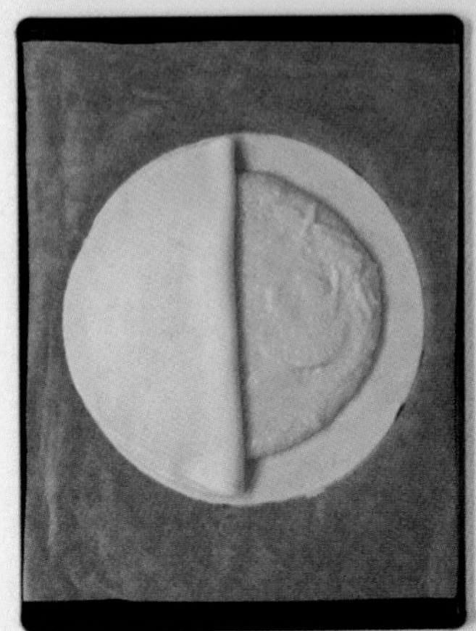

5 6

7 8

5	Spread the frangipan mixture over the first circle of pastry, stopping a good inch short of the edge.	6	Cover with the second pastry circle, pressing firmly to seal the edges all round.
7	Glaze the top of the galette all over with the beaten egg. Use a knife to draw arcs of a circle over the top, working from the center out.	8	Make small nicks with the knife all round the edge of the galette. Prick small holes (and a larger one in the center) over the surface to allow the air to escape. Chill for 30 minutes.

9	Transfer the galette to the very hot oven. When it has risen well (about 15 minutes), reduce the temperature to 400°F. Continue to bake for about a further 20 minutes. Serve warm or at room temperature.	**FREEZING ADVICE** You can put the unbaked galette on a plate (without glazing or decorating it). Leave to harden in the freezer for 12 hours before popping it into a freezer bag. Seal well. When you are ready to bake it, glaze and decorate the galette before putting it in the oven still frozen. Allow a further 10 minutes' baking time.

TIRAMISU

SERVES 6–8 • PREPARATION: 25 MINUTES • SETTING: 6 HOURS

1 cup freshly made strong black coffee
⅓ cup sugar
5 eggs
2 cups mascarpone (Italian-style heavy cream)
10 oz sponge fingers (ladyfinger biscuits) (you need about 35)
2 tablespoons unsweetened cocoa powder

IN ADVANCE:
Pour the hot coffee into a bowl. Add 1 teaspoon of the sugar, mix, and set aside to cool.

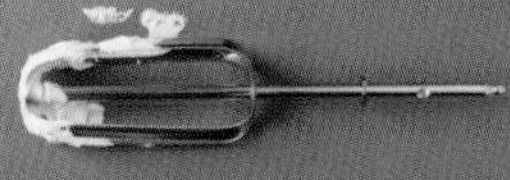

1 2

3 4

1	Separate the eggs. Beat the yolks with the remaining sugar until the mixture is pale and creamy.	2	Add the mascarpone and beat with an electric beater until the mixture is light and fluffy.	
3	Whip the egg whites to a supple, not too firm, meringue.	4	Add the whites in two batches into the cream mixture, folding them in with a flexible spatula.	➢

5

6

5	Very quickly dip several sponge fingers, one by one, in the coffee and, before they lose their shape, use them to line the base of a large square dish or mold in a single layer.	6	Cover with a thin layer of the cream mixture. Build up two more layers of sponge fingers and cream in this way. Cover the dish with plastic wrap and refrigerate for at least 6 hours.

7	Just before serving, sift the unsweetened cocoa powder through a small strainer over the surface of the tiramisu.	**TIP** ❊ The sponge fingers become oversoft if you leave them too long in the coffee: you want to soften them but not make them soggy.

39

MASCARPONE CHEESECAKE

SERVES 10–12 • PREPARATION: 20 MINUTES • COOKING: 1 HOUR 15 MINUTES • RESTING: 3 HOURS MINIMUM

FOR THE BASE:
4 oz graham crackers
6 tablespoons butter
⅛ cup + 1 tablespoon sugar

FOR THE TOPPING:
1½ cups cream cheese + 1 cup sugar
1 scant cup mascarpone (Italian-style heavy cream)
3 eggs + 1 teaspoon vanilla extract

IN ADVANCE:
Preheat the oven to 300°F. Put a rack in the center with a second just below and place a shallow dish or bowl on this lower shelf.

1

3

4

5

6

1	Whiz the crackers for 30–60 seconds in the bowl of a mixer fitted with a blade to make fine crumbs.	2	Place the butter in a small pan and melt. Remove from the heat.	3	Mix the sugar with the cracker crumbs in a bowl.	
4	Pour over the melted butter and mix into the cracker crumbs with a fork.	5	Spread this mixture over the base of an 8-inch springform cake pan.	6	Firm the crumbs then refrigerate the pan for 5–10 minutes.	➢

7 8
9 10

7	Put the cream cheese with the sugar in the bowl of a mixer fitted with a blade. Beat for 1 minute until the cheese is softened.	8	Add the mascarpone and mix again for 10–20 seconds. Remove the lid and scrape down the sides with a flexible spatula.
9	Add the eggs, one at a time, mixing well before adding the next. Scrape down the sides again then add the vanilla extract and mix briefly.	10	Remove the pan from the fridge and pour the cream topping over the cracker base.

11	Fill the shallow dish or bowl on the lower oven rack with very hot water. Transfer the cheesecake to the upper rack of the oven. Bake for 1 hour 15 minutes or until the middle of the cheesecake is no longer runny.	**SETTING** Remove the cheesecake from the oven and let cool on a wire rack. Once cool, cover with plastic wrap and leave to set in the fridge for at least 3 hours before serving. It will reach its ideal consistency after 12 hours.

CORSICAN CHEESECAKE

SERVES 6–8 • PREPARATION: 20 MINUTES • COOKING: 45 MINUTES

2 cups drained ricotta or brocciù (ewe's milk cheese), if you can find it
olive oil, for greasing
peel of 1 untreated lemon

5 eggs
⅔ cup sugar
½ teaspoon eau-de-vie
pinch of salt

IN ADVANCE:
Drain the ricotta (if necessary) for 1 hour. Oil a 10-inch cake pan. Zest the lemon. Preheat the oven to 350°F.

1	Separate the eggs.	2	Beat the yolks with the sugar using an electric beater, until pale.	3	Add the ricotta in two goes. Mix in with a hand whisk. Add the lemon peel then the eau-de-vie.
4	Whip the egg whites with the salt until they form firm peaks.	5	Use a flexible spatula to incorporate the whites with the ricotta mixture.	6	Do not overmix; use the spatula gently. ➢

7	Pour the mixture into the prepared pan and lightly smooth the surface with a spatula.	**TIP** ☛ In this recipe you can incorporate the egg whites with less concern for them flattening because this mixture does not need to be too light and fluffy.

8	Transfer the pan to the oven and bake for 45 minutes. Remove and let cool on a wire rack. Cover and refrigerate before serving.

TO SERVE

This cheesecake should be served chilled. You can serve it with a red berry compote or a fresh coulis.

NOTE

This cheesecake originates in Corsica, France, where it is called Fiadone. Brocciù is a soft white cheese made from ewe's milk, and is considered the island's national cheese. If you cannot find it, use ricotta. The cheesecake is flavored with Mirto, a myrtle-flavored liqueur, also made in Corsica. You can use an eau-de-vie of your choice.

41

JELLY ROLL

SERVES 8 • PREPARATION: 40 MINUTES • COOKING: 10 MINUTES

SPONGE:
3 tablespoons butter
4 egg yolks + 3 egg whites
⅓ cup sugar + 1 teaspoon extra
¾ cup self-rising flour

VANILLA SYRUP:
5 tablespoons water
¼ cup sugar
½ teaspoon vanilla extract
8 oz strawberry preserve

IN ADVANCE:
Preheat the oven to 475°F. Cover a cookie sheet measuring 16 x 12 inches with parchment paper.

1	Begin by making the sponge. Melt the butter in a small pan.	2	Use a little of the melted butter to grease the parchment paper.	3	With an electric beater, beat the egg yolks with the ⅓ cup of sugar for 5 minutes on medium.
4	Gently incorporate the flour using a flexible spatula; do not overmix.	5	Whip the egg whites, adding the teaspoon of sugar once they start to hold their shape.	6	Add the egg whites and the melted butter to the yolks. ➢

7 8
9 10

7	Gently mix everything together before very carefully pouring the mixture onto the cookie sheet—try not to burst the air bubbles.	8	Spread the mixture over the entire sheet using a palette knife.
9	Transfer to the oven and bake for 7 minutes, until the top is lightly colored.	10	Remove the sponge from the oven and invert it immediately onto a lightly oiled pastry board.

11 Peel off the parchment paper, cover the sponge with a clean dish towel (keeping it moist will prevent it breaking when rolled), and let cool.

TIP

Spread the sponge mixture with smooth strokes to get it uniformly thick, about ¼ inch maximum. Otherwise, thinner parts will dry out during baking.

NOTE

☛ Go easy with the spatula or you will break the air bubbles in the mixture. These are what give the sponge its light texture.

➢

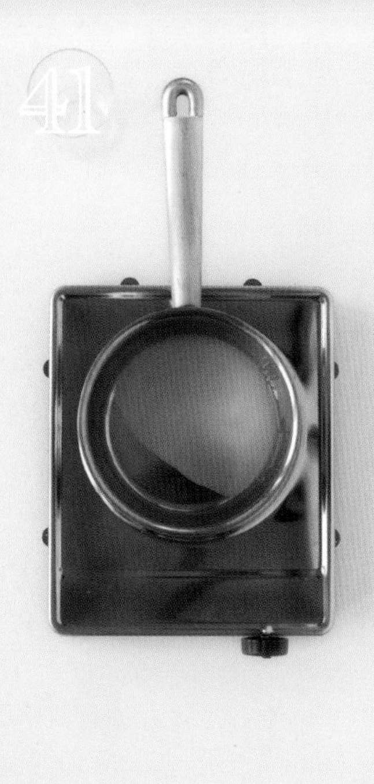

12

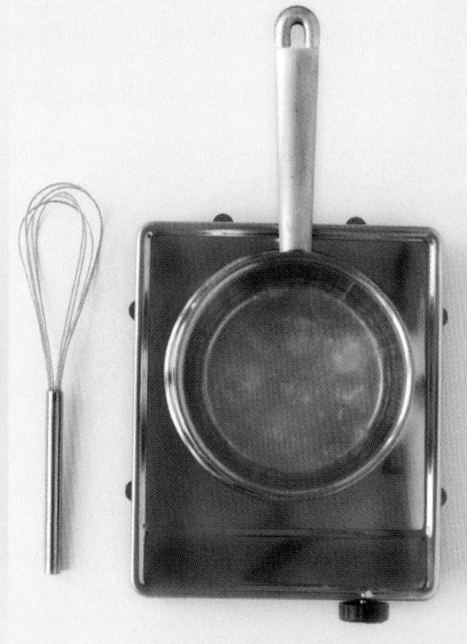

13

14

15

16

17

12	Pour the water into a small pan then add the sugar. Heat gently.	13	Dissolve the sugar, stirring with a whisk, then bring to a boil and remove from the heat immediately.	14	Let the syrup cool then add the vanilla extract and mix well.
15	Spread the syrup over the sponge with a pastry brush then spoon on preserve.	16	Use all but 2 tablespoons of preserve to cover the sponge, then roll it up tightly.	17	Gently melt the reserved strawberry preserve with 1 tablespoon water.

18	Use the pastry brush to cover the jelly roll completely with the thinned preserve.	**STORAGE** The jelly roll will keep in the fridge for up to 4 days.
OPTION 1		**OPTION 2**
Make the sponge in advance and roll it up with its parchment paper immediately you take it out of the oven. Wrap in plastic wrap.		You can make a narrower roll (like a log), in which case only cover two-thirds or half of the width of the cookie sheet with the sponge mixture.

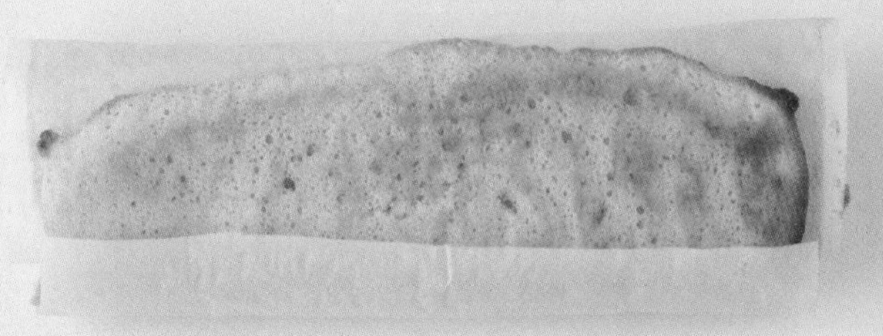

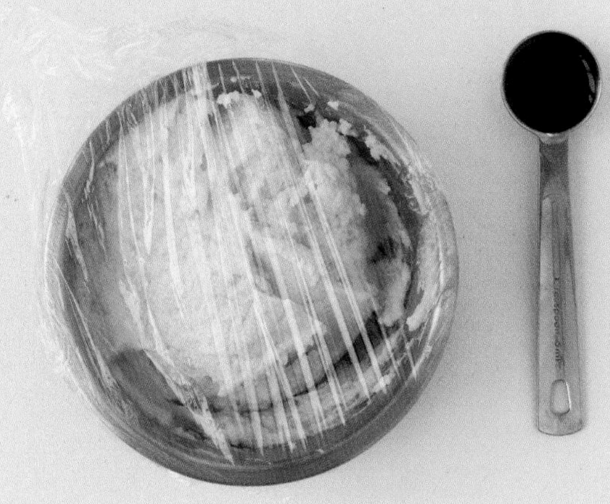

COFFEE LOG

SERVES 10 • PREPARATION: 20 MINUTES • COOKING: 5 MINUTES • RESTING: 1 HOUR

1 baked Jelly Roll (see recipe 41) measuring about 8 inches
10 oz coffee-flavored Butter Cream (see recipe 03)

COFFEE SYRUP:
¼ cup sugar
5 tablespoons water
¼ teaspoon coffee extract

1 2

3 4

1	Dissolve the sugar in the water over a gentle heat. Bring to a boil, remove from the heat, and let cool. Stir in the coffee extract.	2	Brush the cooled syrup over the surface of the prepared sponge, then spread three-quarters of the butter cream over it.
3	Roll up the sponge as tightly as possible, starting from the shorter side.	4	Cover the log with the remaining cream using a spatula. Refrigerate for 1 hour before serving.

43

POPPYSEED CAKE

SERVES 12 • PREPARATION: 35 MINUTES • COOKING: 35 MINUTES

1 oz raisins + a little rum for soaking
13 oz Sweet Pie Pastry (see recipe 66)
4 tablespoons butter
13 oz poppyseeds
⅞ cup sugar
2 tablespoons honey
⅛ cup ground almonds
¼ oz or 1 sachet vanilla sugar
peel of 1 lemon
2 egg whites + 1 whole egg for glazing

IN ADVANCE:
Preheat the oven to 350°F.

1 2

3 4

1	Cover the raisins with rum and leave to swell. Butter a 9-in square cake pan, or its rectangular equivalent.	2	Thinly roll out the pastry into two sheets the size of your pan.	
3	Place one sheet in the base of the cake pan.	4	Melt the butter in a small pan. Remove from the heat and set aside.	➢

5	Run the poppyseeds through a coffee grinder in batches and tip them into a large bowl.	6	Add the sugar and mix well to combine.	7	Stir in the melted butter, then add the honey and mix again.
8	Incorporate the ground almonds along with the vanilla sugar.	9	Lastly, add the lemon peel and the drained raisins.	10	Whip the egg whites until firm and stiff.

11 12

13 14

11	Gently incorporate the whipped whites into the poppyseed mixture.	12	Tip the mixture into the cake pan to cover the pastry base.
13	Place the second sheet of pastry on top. Glaze the pastry with the beaten egg.	14	Bake in the oven for 35 minutes. Serve cut into squares.

44

CHOCOLATE CHARLOTTE

SERVES 6–8 • PREPARATION: 15 MINUTES • RESTING: 3 HOURS

1 lb 4 oz Chocolate Mousse (see recipe 06)
butter, for greasing
4 tablespoons water
4 tablespoons sugar syrup
25 sponge fingers (ladyfinger biscuits)

IN ADVANCE:
Prepare the chocolate mousse and keep in the fridge.

1 2

3 4

1	Butter the base of a 6-inch charlotte mold. Cut out a circle of parchment paper to fit the base, butter it, and place it, butter-side up.	2	Mix together the water and syrup in a shallow dish.	
3	Reserving 10 of the sponge fingers for the top, quickly dip the remainder, one by one, in the sweetened water.	4	Use the sponge fingers to line the sides of the mold, with the rounded face of the fingers touching the sides.	➢

5 6

7 8

5	Continue to line the mold with all the sponge fingers in this way. Leave the base clear.	6	Pour the chocolate mousse into the center of the dish.
7	Quickly dip the reserved 10 sponge fingers in the sweetened water and use them to cover the top of the mousse.	8	Place two plates the size of the mold on top of the charlotte. Cover everything in plastic wrap and refrigerate for 3 hours.

	TO TURN OUT THE CHARLOTTE	TO SERVE
9	Unwrap the charlotte and remove the plates. Dip the base of the mold into very hot water, put a serving plate on top, and invert the mold. Gently remove the circle of parchment paper and serve immediately.	Serve the chocolate charlotte with vanilla custard (see recipe 01), decorated with grated chocolate if you wish.

VACHERIN

SERVES 6 • PREPARATION: 55 MINUTES • COOKING: 1 HOUR 30 MINUTES • FREEZING: 2 HOURS

FRENCH MERINGUE:
3 egg whites
the same weight in both superfine sugar and confectioners' sugar (about 3½ oz of each)
17 fl oz vanilla ice cream
17 fl oz strawberry ice cream
about 2 cups Chantilly Cream (see recipe 14)
fresh fruit, to decorate
about 2 cups Red Berry Compote (see recipe 13), to serve

IN ADVANCE:
Preheat the oven to 195°F or to its coolest setting.

1 2

3 4

1	To make the meringue, whip the egg whites in a large bowl. Add the superfine sugar once the whites hold their shape.	2	Whip again until the egg whites are firm. Sift over the confectioners' sugar using a fine sieve and incorporate with a flexible spatula.
3	Draw two 5-inch circles (use a small deep pan as a guide) on parchment paper lining a cookie sheet. Using a piping bag, fill both circles almost to the edge with meringue.	4	Pipe four sticks of meringue next to the spirals. Bake for 1 hour 30 minutes. Take the ice cream from the freezer 10–20 minutes before the end of cooking. ➢

5	Use the same pan that served as a guide for the meringue circles and line the interior with plastic wrap, allowing plenty to overlap the sides.	6	Turn out the two ice creams into separate bowls and work with a spoon to soften them.
7	When the meringue has cooled completely, place one disc in the base of the pan.	8	Spoon in the softened ice creams and fill almost to the top.

9

Cover the ice cream with the second meringue disc. Place the pan in the freezer and leave to harden for at least 2 hours.

TIP

☛ Be sure to make the meringue discs slightly smaller than the diameter of your pan so that you can slip them into it without breaking. Don't make them too small, though: the pan serves as a mold for assembling the vacherin and the meringues must be tailored to fit.

➢

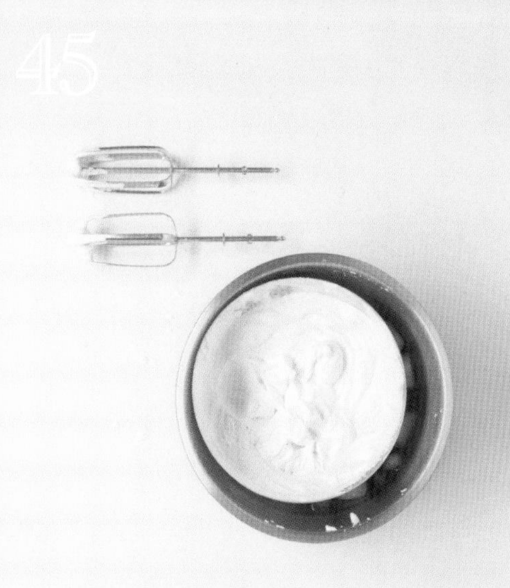

10 11

12 13

10	One hour before serving, cut the meringue sticks into fingers the height of the vacherin. Prepare the Chantilly (see recipe 14).	11	Remove the pan from the freezer. Use the plastic wrap to help you lift the vacherin out of the pan. Discard the plastic wrap.
12	Place the vacherin on a serving plate. Cover the sides with a thick layer of Chantilly, smoothing it with a spatula.	13	Arrange the meringue fingers around the sides of the vacherin. Return it to the freezer for 15–30 minutes to ensure the fingers stick to the Chantilly.

		VARIATION
14	Keep the remaining Chantilly in the fridge. When you are ready to serve, spread a layer of the cream on top of the vacherin and pipe a few little swirls on top. Decorate with a few fresh fruits and serve with the compote.	Use caramel and chocolate ice cream instead of the vanilla and strawberry. Serve the vacherin with salty butter caramel sauce (see recipe 10).

LITTLE CAKES

French meringues ... 46
Blueberry muffins ... 47
Chocolate muffins ... 48
Banana muffins ... 49
Bran & raisin muffins ... 50
Oat & apple muffins ... 51
Madeleines ... 52
Chocolate macaroons ... 53
Raspberry macaroons ... 54
Caramel macaroons ... 55
Star buns ... 56
Doughnuts ... 57
Maple syrup glaze ... 58
Chocolate chip cookies ... 59
Almost Oreos® ... 60
Biscuits ... 61
Pecan cookies ... 62
Breton cookies ... 63
Blueberry pancakes ... 64
Eggy bread ... 65

FRENCH MERINGUES

MAKES 8 OZ MERINGUE • PREPARATION: 10 MINUTES • COOKING: 1 HOUR 30 MINUTES TO 2 HOURS

3 egg whites
the same weight in both superfine sugar and confectioners' sugar (about 3½ oz of each)

IN ADVANCE:
Preheat the oven to 195°F or set to its lowest temperature. Cover a baking sheet with parchment paper.

1 2

3 4

1	Whip the egg whites in a large bowl. Add the superfine sugar once the whites hold their shape.	2	Whip again until the whites are fully firm. Sift over the confectioners' sugar and incorporate with a flexible spatula.
3	Drop dessertspoonfuls of meringue on the baking sheet, spaced apart. Transfer to the oven and bake for 1 hour 30 minutes to 2 hours.	4	Once cooked, switch off the oven and leave the meringues inside to cool, with the door closed. They will easily peel off the paper.

BLUEBERRY MUFFINS

MAKES 6 MUFFINS • PREPARATION: 15 MINUTES • COOKING: 25 MINUTES

2 tablespoons butter
1 egg
⅓ cup sugar
½ cup crème fraîche or sour cream

1 cup flour
½ teaspoon salt
1 teaspoon baking powder
¾ cup frozen blueberries

IN ADVANCE:
Preheat the oven to 350°F. Grease 6 individual muffin pans or a 6-hole tray.

1

2

1	Melt the butter then remove from the heat. Beat the egg with the sugar until light and creamy. Add the melted butter and mix in with a whisk, then add the crème fraîche or sour cream in two lots.	2	Mix the flour, salt, and baking powder in a bowl. Remove the blueberries from the freezer and mix them with the flour. Make a well in the center then tip in the liquid ingredients and stir rapidly.	➢

3	Fill the molds two-thirds full with the batter (work quickly so that the blueberries do not defrost) then tap the pans or tray on the counter top to settle the mixture. Transfer to the oven and bake for 25 minutes (or for 15 minutes for smaller ones).	**TIP** ☛ Make sure you do not overwork the mixture, which tends to make the muffins hard. Do not fill the molds right to the top, so that the batter rises into a pleasing dome top.

4	Remove the muffins from the oven, run the blade of a knife around each one then leave to cool in the molds for 10 minutes before turning out onto a wire rack.	**TO SERVE** Enjoy these muffins for breakfast, with a pat of butter and served with tea or coffee.

CHOCOLATE MUFFINS

VARIATION ON BLUEBERRY MUFFINS

Sift 1 cup flour, 2 tablespoons unsweetened cocoa powder, and ½ teaspoon baking powder in a bowl. In a second bowl, beat ⅓ cup sugar with 2 eggs. Add 8 tablespoons warm melted butter then 6 tablespoons milk. Pour this mixture onto the flour and lightly mix, incorporating 2 oz dark chocolate, chopped into chips, at the end.

BANANA MUFFINS

VARIATION ON BLUEBERRY MUFFINS

Sift 1⅛ cups flour, ½ teaspoon baking soda, ½ teaspoon baking powder, ½ teaspoon powdered cinnamon, and a pinch of salt in a bowl. In a second bowl, beat ⅔ cup sugar with 1 egg. Add 3 tablespoons warm melted butter, 2 small ripe mashed bananas and 2 tablespoons milk. Pour this mixture onto the dry ingredients and lightly incorporate.

BRAN & RAISIN MUFFINS

VARIATION ON BLUEBERRY MUFFINS

Soak 3 oz All-Bran® in 1 scant cup of milk. In a large bowl, beat ½ cup golden granulated sugar with 1 egg, add 4 tablespoons sunflower oil in a stream, then ¼ teaspoon vanilla extract. Stir in the All-Bran® and milk. In a second bowl, mix together ⅞ cup of flour, ¼ teaspoon baking soda and a pinch of salt. Add the liquid ingredients and lightly mix, incorporating ½ cup of raisins at the end.

OAT & APPLE MUFFINS

VARIATION ON BLUEBERRY MUFFINS

Soak 1 cup rolled oats in ¾ cup of milk. Beat ¼ cup golden granulated sugar with 1 egg, then pour in 3 tablespoons melted butter and ¼ teaspoon vanilla extract. In another bowl, mix together 1 cup of flour, ¼ teaspoon baking powder, a pinch of powdered cinnamon, and a pinch of salt. Add the liquid ingredients and lightly mix, incorporating 1 cup diced apple at the end.

MADELEINES

MAKES 18 • PREPARATION: 20 MINUTES • COOKING: 10 MINUTES • RESTING: AT LEAST 2 HOURS

2 whole eggs + 1 egg yolk
5 tablespoons butter
½ vanilla bean
⅓ cup sugar
½ cup flour
½ teaspoon baking powder
½ teaspoon salt

IN ADVANCE:
Beat the eggs and the yolk together in a bowl.

1	Melt the butter and keep warm over a low heat.	2	Add the seeds scraped from the vanilla bean to the eggs with the sugar and beat well.	3	Mix the flour with the baking powder and salt.	
4	Sprinkle the flour over the egg mixture and mix with a flexible spatula until evenly blended.	5	Pour on the warm butter in a stream while continuing to mix with the spatula.	6	Cover the batter and rest in a cool place for at least 2 hours (and up to 12 hours).	➢

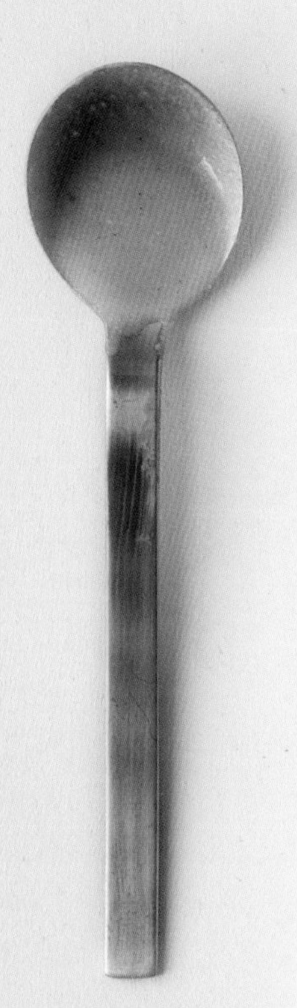

		TIPS
7	Preheat the oven to 400°F. Carefully butter then flour an 8-hole madeleine pan. Shake the tin to remove the surplus. Spoon the batter into the molds and fill almost level to the top.	While the batter is resting it is best to cover it with plastic wrap placed directly on the surface. If you have nonstick molds, there is no need to butter and flour them. Note: the oven must be very hot if the madeleines are to rise and cook before they dry out.

8	Transfer to the oven for about 10 minutes.

TURNING OUT

Turn out the madeleines once they come out of the oven, then put them back in their molds to cool. Let them cool completely before eating.

TIP

☛ After 2–3 minutes the rims of the madeleines should be a little risen. Reduce the oven temperature to 325°F and continue to cook for about 8 minutes, or until the madeleines are golden brown.

53

CHOCOLATE MACAROONS

MAKES 10 • PREPARATION: 25 MINUTES • COOKING: 11 MINUTES • RESTING: AT LEAST 20 MINUTES

FOR THE MACAROONS:
¼ cup ground almonds
⅝ cup confectioners' sugar
1 scant tablespoon unsweetened cocoa powder
1 egg white
1 tablespoon superfine sugar
2 drops red food coloring
3½ oz Chocolate Ganache (see recipe 07)

IN ADVANCE:
Prepare a baking sheet covered with silicone paper.

1 2
3 4

1	Whiz the ground almonds, confectioners' sugar, and unsweetened cocoa powder in a mixer until fine. Stop the motor and stir with a spatula to prevent the powder from sticking.	2	Sift the powder through a fine-mesh strainer.
3	Whip the egg whites. When they begin to hold their shape, gradually add the sugar and continue to whip until the whites are firm.	4	Add the food coloring, drop by drop, and mix gently with a flexible spatula until the color is uniform. ➢

5 6

7 8

5	Sprinkle the dry ingredients a little at a time on the meringue, incorporating each addition with the flexible spatula.	6	Work carefully. You want to end up with an evenly blended mixture.
7	Fill a piping bag and form small macaroons, well spaced on the prepared baking sheet. Tap the sheet on the counter top. Preheat the oven to 325°F on fan setting, if possible.	8	Leave the macaroons in the warmest part of the room to form a crust (it can take several hours if the air is damp). Press lightly on one macaroon to check that it no longer sticks.

9

Transfer to the oven and bake for 11 minutes for small macaroons, or for 15 minutes for medium ones.

TIP

☛ Wait until the macaroons are cold before peeling them from the paper.

FILLING

Put a pat of ganache in the center of the flat side of a macaroon shell then press the flat side of a second macaroon onto the ganache. Press together until the ganache spreads out to the sides.

54

RASPBERRY MACAROONS

VARIATION ON CHOCOLATE MACAROONS

Prepare the macaroons, following recipe 53, omitting the cocoa powder and tinting the egg whites with 6 drops of red food coloring. Instead of filling with ganache, use raspberry preserve.

CARAMEL MACAROONS

VARIATION ON CHOCOLATE MACAROONS

Prepare the macaroons, following recipe 53, but with ½ teaspoon unsweetened cocoa powder and tinting the egg whites with 1 drop of red food coloring and 1 drop of yellow. Instead of filling with ganache, use 3½ oz salty butter caramel sauce (see recipe 10).

STAR BUNS

MAKES 8 • PREPARATION: 20 MINUTES • COOKING: 1 HOUR 15 MINUTES • RESTING: 12 HOURS

1 cup milk
1 vanilla bean
½ cup golden granulated sugar
½ cup flour

1 whole egg + 1 egg yolk
2 tablespoons butter
2 teaspoons rum

IN ADVANCE:
Split the vanilla bean in two and scrape out the seeds into the milk.

1	Heat the milk in a small pan with vanilla seeds and the split bean.	2	Mix the sugar with the flour in a bowl with a pouring lip.	3	Add the eggs and mix with a wooden spoon.	
4	Remove the bean from the milk and reserve. Pour the milk over the eggs, stirring with the wooden spoon.	5	Add the butter, cut into cubes. Continue to stir until it melts.	6	Replace the vanilla bean in the mixture.	➢

7 8
9 10

7	Let the mixture cool to room temperature before adding the rum. Stir and cover with plastic wrap. Refrigerate for at least 12 hours.	8	Take the batter from the fridge 1 hour before you want to cook. Preheat the oven to its highest setting and put a rack in the center.
9	Whisk the batter until it is evenly blended again and remove the vanilla bean.	10	Place your molds on a baking sheet and fill them three-quarters full or to within ½ inch of the top. Transfer them to the oven.

		TIP
11	Let the batter expand and color (about 10 minutes). When the buns are nicely golden-brown, reduce the temperature to 350°F. Continue to cook until the visible part is dark brown and feels firm when pressed with a finger (this takes 60–70 minutes). Let them cool before turning them out of the molds.	☛ For preference, use an 8-hole star-shaped silicon tray if you can find one, rather than a metal one. Alternatively, a small silicon muffin pan or individual molds could be used.

DOUGHNUTS

→ MAKES 12 • PREPARATION: 30 MINUTES • COOKING: 5 MINUTES ←

4 tablespoons butter
5 cups all-purpose flour + extra for dusting
⅞ cup sugar
2 teaspoons baking powder
1 teaspoon baking soda
2 teaspoons salt
1 teaspoon freshly powdered nutmeg
¾ cup buttermilk
2 whole eggs + 1 egg yolk

CINNAMON SUGAR:

⅔ cup sugar +
½ teaspoon powdered cinnamon

IN ADVANCE:

Once the batter is almost ready, heat 1¾ pints peanut oil in a Dutch oven over a medium to high heat, or preheat a deep fryer to 375°F.

1 2

3 4

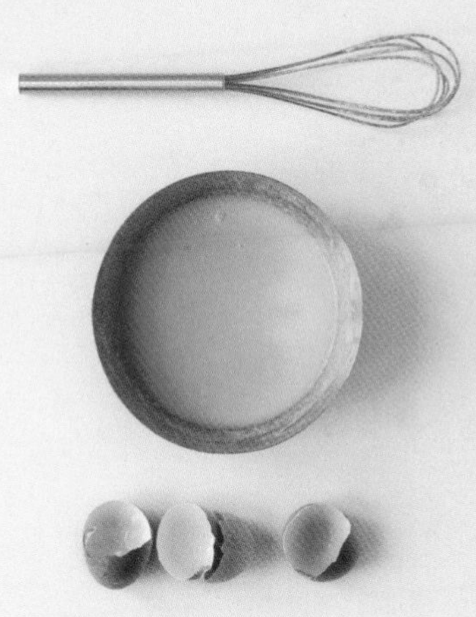

1	First prepare the cinnamon sugar by mixing the ingredients together then tip onto a plate.	2	Melt the butter. Let cool.
3	In a large bowl, use a whisk to mix together 1½ cups of the flour with the sugar, baking powder, baking soda, salt, and nutmeg.	4	In a separate bowl, mix the buttermilk with the eggs and egg yolk. Beat, add the melted butter, and beat again. ➢

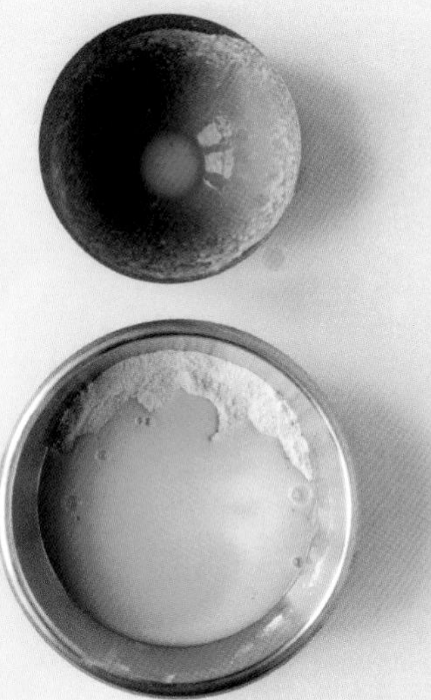

5 6
7 8

5	Pour this mixture over the dry ingredients.	6	Beat with a wooden spoon until the mixture is evenly blended.
7	Add the remaining flour and mix again until it is fully incorporated.	8	Place the dough on a well-floured board and roll out using a floured rolling pin until the dough is about ½ inch in thickness.

9	Use 2 floured cookie cutters, one 3½ inches and the other 1 inch in diameter, to make rings. Place them on a large plate. Gather up the trimmings and work them quickly into a ball then flatten. Roll out as before to make more doughnuts until all the dough is used up.	**TIP** ☛ The doughnut dough is very sticky, which is why you need to liberally flour the board, rolling pin, and cutters to ensure your rings are evenly shaped.

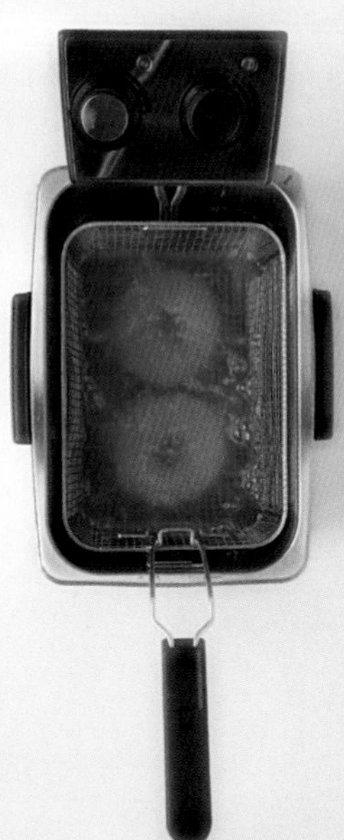

10 11

12 13

10	Carefully lower the doughnuts into the hot oil, as many as possible without them overlapping.	11	When they rise to the surface and are nicely golden (this takes about 2 minutes), turn them over using a slotted spoon.
12	Let them cook for 1 further minute.	13	Remove the doughnuts using the slotted spoon when they are golden on the second side.

14	Drain them on a raised wire rack or on kitchen paper. Let the oil return to temperature before frying another batch. Meanwhile, turn the hot doughnuts in the cinnamon sugar.	**TIP** ☛ If you don't have a deep fryer, it is best to use a Dutch oven which retains the heat well, so that the oil will not cool too much between batches.

MAPLE SYRUP GLAZE

ENOUGH FOR 12 DOUGHNUTS • PREPARATION: 5 MINUTES

½ cup confectioners' sugar
about 3 tablespoons maple syrup

Sift the confectioners' sugar into a small bowl. Pour the maple syrup over the confectioners' sugar.

Beat vigorously.

GLAZING	TIPS
Trickle the glaze over the doughnuts and spread with a small spatula. Wait a few minutes for the glaze to set. You can also pour the glaze onto a plate or shallow dish and dip the doughnuts in one by one before leaving them to drain over the plate. Place them on a wire rack.	For a more runny glaze, add up to 2 teaspoons extra maple syrup. Take care not to make fingerprints: this glaze does not set completely.

CHOCOLATE CHIP COOKIES

MAKES 12 • PREPARATION: 25 MINUTES • RESTING: 10 MINUTES • COOKING: 14 MINUTES

5 tablespoons butter
3½ oz dark chocolate (minimum 52% cocoa solids)
½ cup golden granulated sugar
¼ cup superfine sugar

1 egg yolk at room temperature
½ teaspoon vanilla extract
1 cup self-rising flour
½ teaspoon baking soda
½ teaspoon salt

IN ADVANCE:
Preheat the oven to 340°F. Put a rack in the center of the oven. Melt the butter in a small pan, remove from the heat, and let cool.

1 2
3 4

1	Cut up the chocolate into chip-size pieces (about 4 from each square).	2	In a large bowl, mix the golden granulated sugar and the superfine sugar.	
3	Add the warm melted butter and beat with an electric whisk until mixed thoroughly.	4	Add the egg and the vanilla extract. Beat again to incorporate.	➢

5 6

7 8

5	Mix together the flour, baking soda, and salt. Add to the liquid ingredients and beat on slow speed, just enough to incorporate the flour.	6	Add the chocolate chips and mix with a flexible spatula to distribute them evenly in the batter.
7	Cover the batter with plastic wrap and refrigerate for 10 minutes. Meanwhile, cover a baking sheet with parchment paper.	8	Remove the batter from the fridge and form into large balls. Use both hands to divide the balls into two with a quick twist. Place them on the baking sheet, uneven side uppermost.

9

Make sure the cookies are well spaced so that they can spread out during cooking. Transfer to the oven and cook for no more than 14 minutes. Let the cookies cool on the baking sheet placed on a wire rack before removing them using a long thin spatula.

HANDY HINTS

On no account try to remove the cookies from the paper as soon as they come out of the oven; you need to wait at least 15 minutes. These cookies stay very soft, even when completely cold. For cookies thicker than shown in the photograph, the melted butter needs to be completely cooled before it is mixed with the sugars (step 3).

ALMOST OREOS®

MAKES 20 • PREPARATION: 25 MINUTES • RESTING: 1 HOUR 45 MINUTES + 30 MINUTES • COOKING: 2 x 12 MINUTES

1 cup + 2 tablespoons all-purpose flour
½ teaspoon salt
1 tablespoon unsweetened cocoa powder
⅓ cup superfine sugar
¼ cup confectioners' sugar
1 oz dark chocolate
½ cup softened butter
1 egg yolk at room temperature
½ teaspoon vanilla extract

GANACHE:
4 oz white chocolate
1 scant cup crème fraîche or sour cream

IN ADVANCE:
Sift together the flour, salt, and unsweetened cocoa powder in a bowl. Mix both sugars in a separate bowl. Melt the dark chocolate over a very gentle heat.

1	Beat the softened butter in a large bowl using an electric beater. Add the sugars and beat again for 1 minute until the mixture is light and fluffy.	2	Scrape the sides of the bowl with a flexible spatula. Add the egg yolk, vanilla extract, and melted chocolate. Beat to incorporate all the ingredients.	
3	Scrape the sides of the bowl again, then add in the dry ingredients.	4	Mix on slow speed, until a dough forms.	➢

5 6
7 8

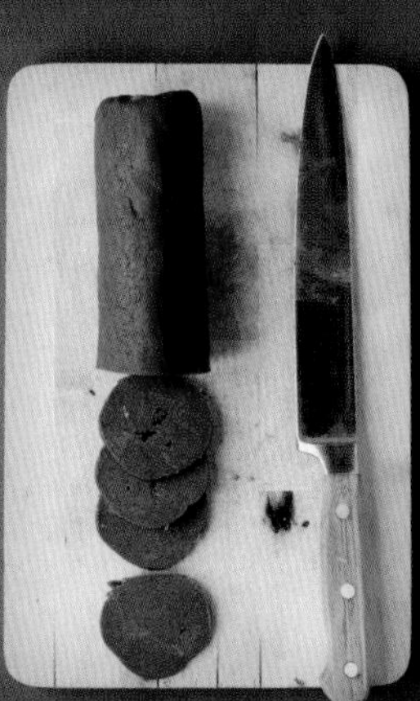

5	Place the dough on a clean board and shape it into a cylinder about 6 inches long.	6	Roll the cylinder on the board to even it out.
7	Cover the dough in plastic wrap and refrigerate for at least 1 hour 30 minutes. Before you remove it, preheat the oven to 325°F. Cover 2 baking sheets with parchment paper.	8	Remove the dough from the fridge and place on a board. Using a sharp knife, trim off the ends then slice the cylinder into 40 very thin rounds (⅛ inch).

9 Place the rounds on the baking sheets and cook them in 2 batches, each for 12 minutes.

COOKING HINT

Cut 20 rounds of the dough and put them on a baking sheet to cook immediately. You can slice the remainder while the first batch is cooling on the baking sheet.

TIPS

☛ If your kitchen is quite warm, cut the cylinder of dough in half and refrigerate one half while you slice the other. It's worth turning the cylinder at regular intervals so that it doesn't flatten on one side under its own weight. The uncooked dough can be kept, wrapped, in the fridge for up to 3 days.

➢

10 11

12 13

10	To make the ganache, first melt the white chocolate over a very gentle heat or in a water bath.	11	Add the crème fraîche or sour cream, mix together, and let cool for about 15 minutes at room temperature.
12	Turn half the cookies upside down on a baking sheet and put a teaspoonful of ganache in the center of each.	13	Top with the remaining cookies and press gently together so that the ganache spreads until you can see it round the sides.

14	Put the assembled cookies in the fridge in a sealed container. Leave them for at least 30 minutes before eating to give the ganache time to set. They will keep for several days stored in this way.

VARIATION

Replace the white chocolate with plain dark chocolate and the crème fraîche or sour cream with whipping cream. Begin by simmering the cream before adding the chocolate, off the heat. Mix together then let cool to room temperature before use.

61

BISCUITS

MAKES 10 • PREPARATION: 20 MINUTES • COOKING: 14 MINUTES

2⅔ cups all-purpose flour + extra for rolling out
3 teaspoons baking powder
large pinch of salt
4 tablespoons cold butter
½ cup raisins, chopped
1 egg
3 tablespoons sugar
⅔ cup light or whipping cream + extra for glazing

IN ADVANCE:
Preheat the oven to 425°F. Cover a baking sheet with parchment paper. Have ready a little flour in a bowl and a little cream for glazing in another.

1 2

3 4

1	Mix the flour, baking powder, and salt in a large bowl. Dice the butter and rub it into the dry ingredients until the mixture forms crumbs.	2	Add the chopped raisins and mix. Make a well in the center.	
3	Beat together the egg and the sugar in a bowl until the mixture is light and creamy. Add the pouring cream and mix again.	4	Pour this mixture into the well. Mix with a flexible spatula until a dough forms.	➢

7	Flour a pastry board and tip the dough on to it. Quickly work the dough until it is even and smooth. Flatten to form a slab at least 1–1¾ inches thick. Flour the top and even out with the rolling pin. Dip a 2-inch round biscuit cutter in the bowl of flour you prepared in advance. Cut out as many biscuits as possible, flouring the cutter between each one.	**TIP** Try to avoid pushing the biscuits out from the cutter; instead, let them drop onto the baking sheet from the cutter by shaking it from the bottom.

8 Glaze the tops of the biscuits with a little cream. Transfer to the oven and cook for 14 minutes. Remove immediately to a wire rack.

BISCUITS AND STRAWBERRY BUTTER

For 20 biscuits: ½ cup softened butter and 3 tablespoons strawberry preserve at room temperature. Beat the soft butter until it becomes pale. Incorporate the preserve and whisk again until it is evenly blended (but not too much; ideally, little specks of strawberry should remain visible. Serve with the warm biscuits.

PECAN COOKIES

MAKES 10 • PREPARATION: 20 MINUTES • COOKING: 20 MINUTES

1 cup all-purpose flour
½ teaspoon salt
½ cup pecan nuts, chopped
½ cup butter softened to a pomade
2 tablespoons sugar
¼ teaspoon vanilla extract
confectioners' sugar for dusting

IN ADVANCE:
Preheat the oven to 340°F. Cover a baking sheet with parchment paper. Mix the flour, salt, and nuts in a bowl.

1 2

3 4

1	Beat the softened butter with the sugar. Add the vanilla then beat in the flour mixture.	2	Work with a flexible spatula until you have a smooth dough.
3	Divide into 10 pieces and shape them into balls the size of a ping-pong ball.	4	Place on the baking sheet. Transfer to the oven and bake for 20 minutes. Let cool on the sheet. Dust with confectioners' sugar to serve.

63

BRETON COOKIES

MAKES 20 • PREPARATION: 30 MINUTES • RESTING: 30 MINUTES • COOKING: 14 MINUTES

½ cup golden granulated sugar
½ cup best-quality salted butter
1 egg yolk at room temperature
½ cup all-purpose flour

IN ADVANCE:
Whiz the sugar in a food mixer for 2–3 minutes to make it finer.

Preheat the oven to 350°F after the dough has rested.

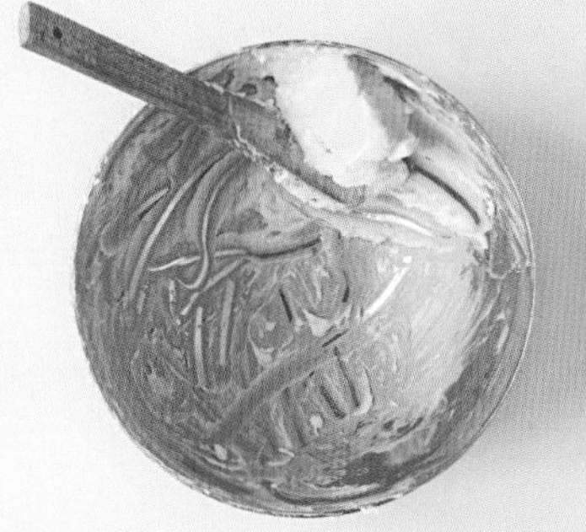

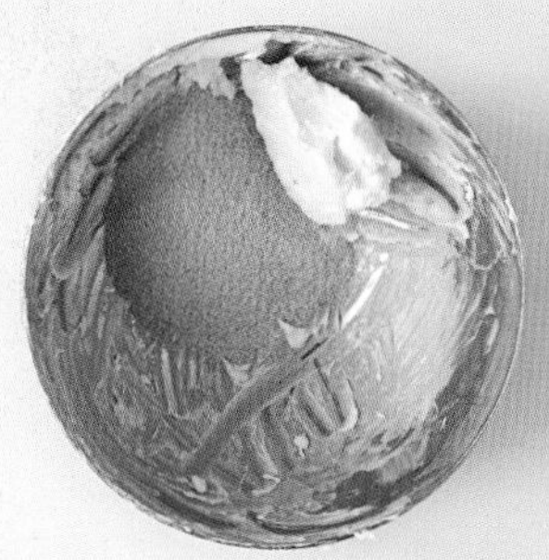

1 2

3 4

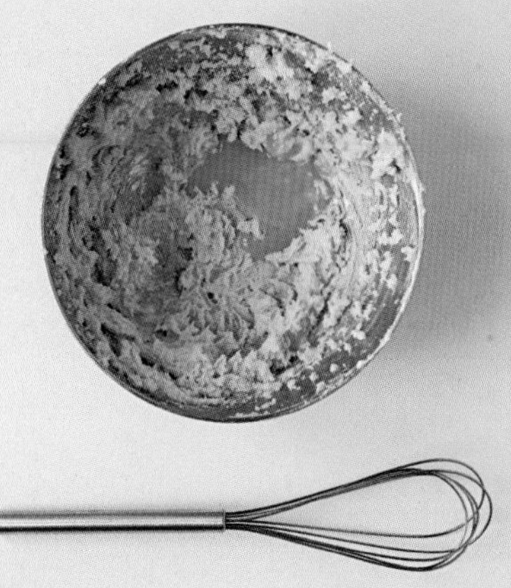

1	Work the butter in a bowl using a wooden spatula until it forms a pomade.	2	Add the sugar and beat with an electric beater, slowly at first, and gradually increasing the speed.	
3	Continue to beat until the mixture is creamy (but not for too long, or the butter will warm up).	4	Add the egg yolk and mix with a whisk just enough to incorporate.	➢

5 6 7

8 9 10

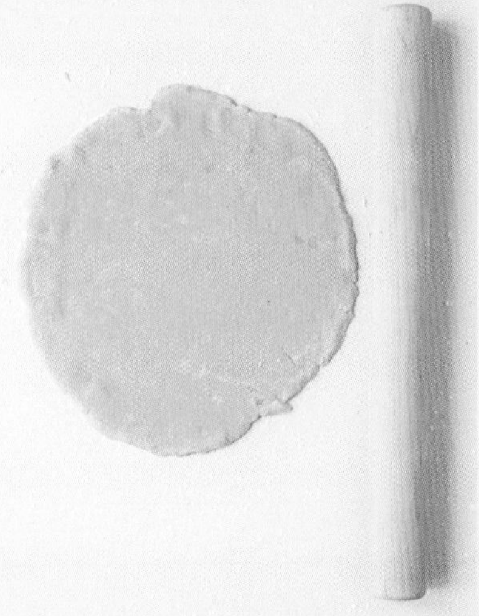

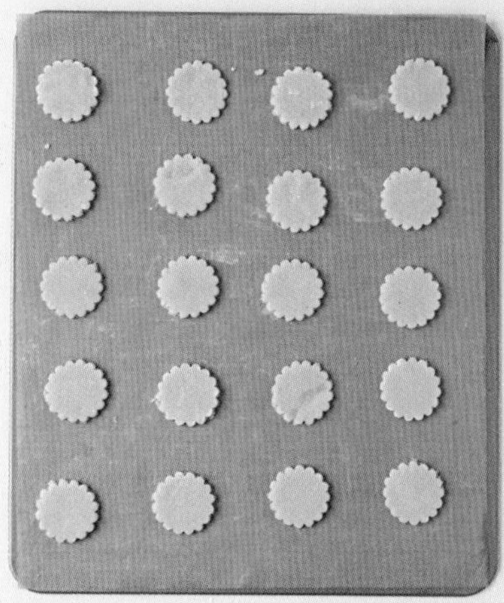

5	Tip in the flour and mix again with the whisk until a dough forms.	6	Quickly work the dough with the palm of your hand until smooth.	7	Shape into a flattened ball and cover in plastic wrap. Refrigerate for 30 minutes.
8	Remove the dough and place on a lightly floured counter top. Roll out to a thickness of ¼ inch.	9	Use a 2-inch fluted cutter to cut out the cookies.	10	Place on a baking sheet covered with parchment paper. Transfer to the oven and cook for 14 minutes.

11	The cookies should be lightly colored. Remove them from the oven and let cool on the baking sheet on a wire rack.	**STORAGE** Store these cookies at room temperature in a tin (not a completely sealed container) so that their moisture can escape. How long they will keep depends on the humidity level of the room.

BLUEBERRY PANCAKES

MAKES 16 • PREPARATION: 15 MINUTES • COOKING: 5 MINUTES

4 tablespoons butter
2 cups + 3 tablespoons milk at room temperature
2 teaspoons lemon juice
1 egg at room temperature
2⅔ cups flour
3 teaspoons or 1 sachet baking powder
1 teaspoon baking soda
2 tablespoons superfine sugar
1 teaspoon salt
1 cup frozen blueberries (keep them frozen)
maple syrup

IN ADVANCE:
Melt the butter in a low-sided skillet. Leave a thin film in the skillet for cooking the pancakes and pour off the rest and reserve it for the batter. Keep the skillet over a low heat while you make the batter.

1	Mix together the milk and the lemon juice.	2	Break the egg into the milk and beat.	3	Add the reserved melted butter and beat again.	
4	Mix together the flour, baking powder, baking soda, sugar, and salt in a large bowl.	5	Make a well in the center. Pour in the liquid ingredients and beat with a hand whisk.	6	Stop as soon as the batter is smooth (overbeating makes the pancakes dry).	➢

7 8

9 10

7	Increase the heat under the skillet to medium. Pour in separate ladlefuls of batter; do not let the pancakes touch as they spread.	8	Remove the blueberries from the freezer and sprinkle generously over the pancakes.
9	Cook until bubbles appear on the surface and the underside is a good pale-brown color (2 minutes at the most).	10	Flip over the pancakes and cook until the second side is also a good color.

11	Remove the pancakes from the skillet and keep warm in the oven at 220°F. Prepare the remainder in batches until all the batter is used up.

TO SERVE

Stack the pancakes on serving plates and drizzle with maple syrup.

TIP

☛ Ideally, have several nonstick skillets heating at the same time so that you can cook all the pancakes in one go. If, however, you are working with a single skillet, dip some kitchen paper in the melted butter prepared for the batter and keep it to hand in a bowl: use this to oil the skillet each time you cook a batch.

EGGY BREAD

SERVES 6 • PREPARATION: 15 MINUTES • COOKING: 5 MINUTES

1 lb unsliced bread (soft batch)
2 eggs
scant 2 cups milk
3 tablespoons superfine sugar
few drops of vanilla extract
4 tablespoons butter
2 bananas
small punnet of strawberries
maple syrup
confectioners' sugar (optional)

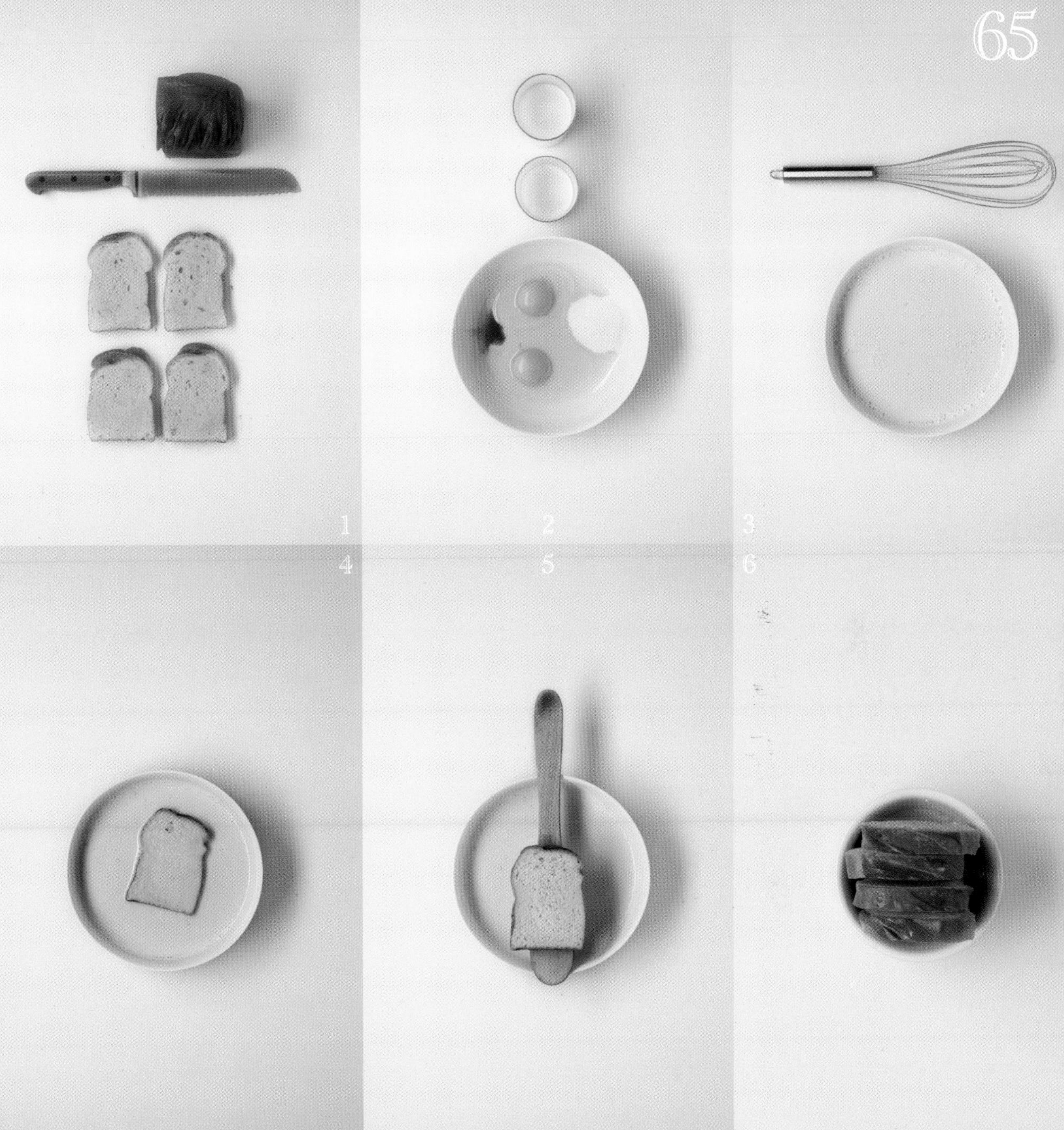

1	Cut the bread into thick slices and lay them flat on the counter top to dry a little.	2	Break the eggs into a large, shallow bowl, then add the milk, sugar, and vanilla.	3	Beat with a hand whisk to mix thoroughly.
4	Dip the bread slices, one at a time, for 10–15 seconds in the egg mixture.	5	Let drain for a few seconds over the bowl.	6	Stack the slices of bread vertically in a second bowl. ➢

7	Heat a pat of the butter in a low-sided skillet over a medium to high heat. When the butter starts to take on color, place as many slices of bread as you can lay flat in the skillet. Cook for 2–3 minutes until the underside is nicely golden.	8	Flip over the slices and cook the other side in the same way for 1–2 minutes.

TIP

☛ Ideally, have several nonstick skillets heating at the same time so that you can cook all the slices simultaneously. If you only have one, heat a fresh pat of butter in the pan to cook the next batch.

9

Serve the egg bread with sliced banana and strawberries, accompanied by maple syrup. Dust with confectioners' sugar if you wish.

HANDY HINT

☛ You can prepare everything several hours in advance: once the ingredients are thoroughly mixed, cover the bowl in plastic wrap and refrigerate.

TARTS

5

Sweet pie pastry 66
Tarte tatin 67
Custard tart 68
Lemon meringue pie 69
Kiwi & mascarpone tartlets 70
Strawberry tartlets 71

SWEET PIE PASTRY

MAKES 13 OZ • PREPARATION: 15 MINUTES • RESTING: 30 MINUTES

½ cup butter
⅞ cup all-purpose flour + extra for dusting
2 tablespoons water

1½ tablespoons sugar
½ teaspoon salt
1 egg

IN ADVANCE:
Cut the butter into cubes and place on the flour on your pastry board.

1 2

3 4

1	Rub the butter into the flour until the mixture resembles breadcrumbs. Make a well in the center. Pour in the water, sugar, salt, and egg.	2	Dissolve the sugar and salt using your finger tips. Work the flour mixture into the liquid in the center; the dough will be fairly wet.
3	Bring in all the remaining flour and squeeze it with both hands. Form a ball but don't overwork it. Flatten into a slab 1–1¾ inches thick and cover in plastic wrap.	4	Refrigerate the dough for at least 30 minutes (flattening the dough speeds up the chilling time) before rolling it out with a rolling pin.

67

TARTE TATIN

SERVES 6–8 • PREPARATION: 25 MINUTES • COOKING: 1 HOUR 20 MINUTES

4 tablespoons water
⅞ cup sugar
4 tablespoons salted butter

2 lb tart green dessert apples
7 oz Sweet Pie Pastry (see recipe 66)

IN ADVANCE:
Preheat the oven to 425°F and put a rack in the center of the oven.

1	Put the water then the sugar into a pan. Beat over a medium heat to dissolve the sugar (see recipe 09).	2	Bring to a boil. As soon as it boils, stop stirring immediately and let the caramel color until it turns amber.	
3	Remove from the heat and add the butter in pieces. Mix with the whisk until the butter is incorporated.	4	Pour the caramel into the base of a 9-inch solid-based cake pan.	➢

67

5 6
7 8

5	Peel and quarter the apples. Remove the cores.	6	Tightly pack the quarters into the pan, peeled side face up. Arrange the remaining quarters on top, filling in the gaps.
7	Transfer to the oven and bake for 1 hour. Remove the pastry from the fridge 15 minutes before the end of the cooking time.	8	Roll out the pastry to a round 9 inches in diameter. Place on top of the apples and bake the tart for a further 15–20 minutes.

9 Remove the tart from the oven. Immediately invert it onto a serving plate. Let cool slightly before serving.

OPTION

Serve the tart warm with some Chantilly cream (see recipe 14) or sour cream.

HANDY HINT

The caramel may crystallize (as shown in the photo for step 4) when you add the butter, but it will melt again in the oven. To prevent it crystallizing, add ½ teaspoon of lemon juice to the sugar–water mix.

CUSTARD TART

SERVES 8 • PREPARATION: 25 MINUTES • COOKING: 50 MINUTES

butter and flour, for preparing the dish
10 oz Sweet Pie Pastry (see recipe 66)
1 egg for glazing

FOR THE CUSTARD:
4 cups milk
1 cup sugar
2 whole eggs + 1 egg yolk
1 cup cornstarch
1 teaspoon vanilla extract + ½ teaspoon salt

IN ADVANCE:
Preheat the oven to 400°F. Grease and flour a square baking dish then lightly tap out the excess flour.

1 2

3 4

1	Roll out the pastry to a thickness of about ⅛ inch and place it in the dish; it should overlap the sides a little.	2	Pinch up the edges of the pastry to make a rim (to stop it shrinking during cooking). Run the rolling pin over the top to trim off the overlap.	
3	Prick the base of the pastry shell with a fork then line the base and sides with lightly buttered baking paper. Bake blind for 10 minutes. Remove the paper.	4	Glaze the pastry with beaten egg then return to the oven for 3–4 minutes to dry. Remove the dish and turn up the temperature to 425°F.	➢

5 6
7 8

5	Pour 2½ cups of the milk into a pan. Add the sugar, stir, and bring to a boil. Beat together the eggs and egg yolk in a bowl.	6	Pour the remaining milk into another bowl, add the cornstarch and whisk immediately. Incorporate the eggs, the vanilla, and the salt.
7	Strain the mixture through a fine-mesh sieve to filter out the bits of yolk casing (which would otherwise coagulate during cooking).	8	When the milk reaches boiling point, remove the pan from the heat. Slowly pour on the egg mixture, whisking well. The cream will thicken.

		VARIATIONS
9	Pour the custard into the tart shell and transfer to the oven for 35 minutes. Remove the tart and place on a wire rack to cool. Cover in plastic wrap and refrigerate to chill completely before serving.	When you are short of time, you can make the custard without its pastry shell. You can also use a sachet of vanilla sugar in place of the vanilla extract, in which case use 2 teaspoons less superfine sugar.

69

LEMON MERINGUE PIE

SERVES 8 • PREPARATION: 30 MINUTES • COOKING: 25 MINUTES • RESTING: 15 MINUTES

13 oz Sweet Pie Pastry (see recipe 66)
12 oz Pastry Cream (see recipe 02), see step 5
½ vanilla bean, split in two
juice and peel of ½ lemon, untreated

2 egg whites
½ cup superfine sugar
2 tablespoons water
⅛ cup confectioners' sugar

IN ADVANCE:
Grease an 11-inch tart pan and place in the fridge.

1	Roll out the pastry in a round a little larger than the diameter of your pan. Prick it all over using a fork.	2	Carefully pick up the pastry and turn it over on the pan so that the pricked side is face down. Line the pan with the pastry, pressing it firmly against the sides.	
3	Run a rolling pin over the top to trim off the overlap. Refrigerate for 15 minutes. Preheat the oven to 340°F.	4	Blind bake the pastry for 20 minutes filled with baking beans then for 10 minutes without the beans. Let cool.	➢

5	Prepare the pastry cream (see recipe 02) by bringing the milk to a boil with the split vanilla bean and its scraped-out seeds.		Add the lemon juice and peel at the end of cooking. Cover with some plastic wrap placed directly on the surface and leave to become completely cold.

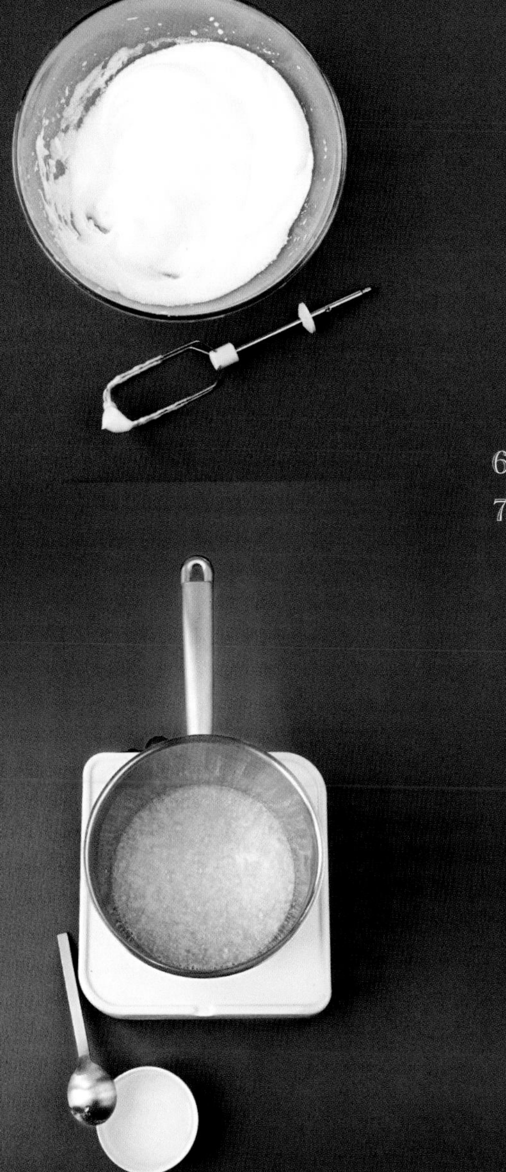

6

7 8

	TO MAKE ITALIAN MERINGUE			
6	Beat the egg whites until stiff, adding a teaspoon of superfine sugar midway through.	8	Boil to the "ball" stage, which takes about 3 minutes. Pour the boiling syrup over the egg whites, letting it run in a stream between the whisk and the sides of the bowl. Beat for about 5 minutes on a slow speed to cool the mixture.	➢
7	Mix the remaining sugar with the water in a pan and bring to a boil.			

9

10

9	Incorporate one-third of the meringue in the pastry cream to lighten its texture. Preheat the broiler.	10	Cover the base of the cooled pastry shell with the pastry cream. Top this with the meringue, making little peaks all over the surface.

11	Sprinkle with confectioners' sugar and flash the pie under the hot broiler (up to 2 minutes) to brown the meringue lightly.	**TIP** ✲ To make peaks on the meringue, lightly strike the surface using the back of a small spoon.

KIWI & MASCARPONE TARTLETS

MAKES 6 • PREPARATION: 30 MINUTES

TART BASE:
3½ oz graham crackers
4 tablespoons butter
2 tablespoons superfine sugar

MASCARPONE FILLING:
¾ cup mascarpone or sour cream
¼ cup confectioners' sugar
½ sachet (½ teaspoon) vanilla sugar

4 kiwifruit

1	Whiz the biscuits in a food mixer for 30–60 seconds to reduce them to crumbs.	**OPTION** You can also crush the biscuits by putting them in a clean dish towel and running a rolling pin over the top. **TIP** ☛ If any large lumps remain, crush them between your fingers.

2 3
4 5

2	Melt the butter in a pan. Mix together the sugar and the crushed biscuits in a bowl, then pour the butter on top.	3	Mix with a fork until the crumbs resemble wet sand.
4	Divide the biscuit crumbs between 6 small pans. Even them out with the back of a spoon and press down with a flat-based object. Smooth the base and sides with the back of the spoon.	5	Put the pans into the fridge to firm up the bases (the butter will solidify). Meanwhile use a fork to beat together the mascarpone or sour cream, confectioners' sugar, and vanilla sugar.

6	Spread the cream mixture over the tartlet bases. Peel the kiwifruit and cut them into slices about ⅓ inch thick. Arrange them, overlapping slightly, on top of the cream. Cover with plastic wrap and refrigerate until ready to serve.	**NOTE** Do not leave the tartlets in the fridge for longer than 2 hours, otherwise the bases will become soggy.

71

STRAWBERRY TARTLETS

MAKES 6 • PREPARATION: 30 MINUTES • COOKING: 10 MINUTES • RESTING: 10 MINUTES

7 oz Sweet Pie Pastry (see recipe 66)
5 oz Almond Cream (see recipe 04)
1 lb 5 oz small strawberries

IN ADVANCE:
Preheat the oven to 425°F.

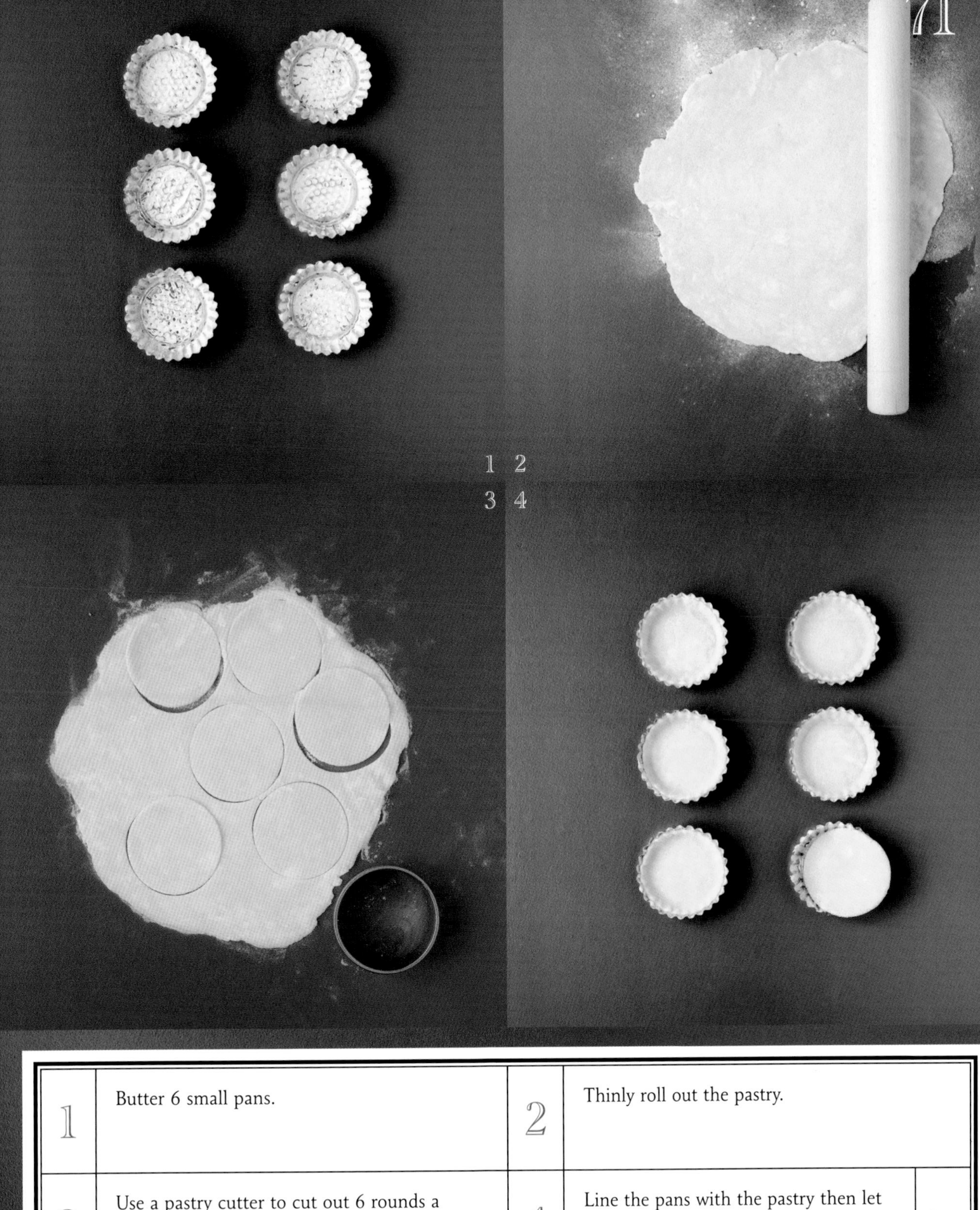

1	Butter 6 small pans.	2	Thinly roll out the pastry.	
3	Use a pastry cutter to cut out 6 rounds a little larger than the diameter of the pans (about 4 inches).	4	Line the pans with the pastry then let them rest in the fridge for 10 minutes.	➢

5 6

7 8

5	Spread the cream over each tartlet shell, smoothing it with the back of a spoon. Transfer to the oven and cook for 10 minutes.	6	Meanwhile, rinse and dry the strawberries on paper towels. Hull them by trimming off the bases.
7	Remove the tartlets from the oven and place on a wire rack to cool.	8	When the tartlets are completely cold, decorate with strawberries.

TIP	OPTION
☛ Choose strawberries that are roughly the same size. Don't use really large ones as they are more difficult to cut with a pastry fork.	You can also thinly slice the strawberries and arrange them, slightly overlapping, in rose fashion. This way, you will use fewer berries.

APPENDICES

GLOSSARY

TABLE OF CONTENTS

INDEX OF RECIPES

INDEX BY INGREDIENTS

ACKNOWLEDGMENTS

GLOSSARY

BALL STAGE

The "ball" describes a stage in cooking sugar. When white sugar is heated its water content evaporates. The temperature of the sugar rises and by degrees it transforms into caramel.

All the stages of this transformation have their technical names recognized and understood by professionals, but only the 'ball' stage is used in this book. In effect, the advanced stages of cooking sugar can be recognized by their color: a caramel that is more or less dark. In contrast, the early stages of cooking sugar show no color; to measure the temperature, either use a sugar thermometer or remove a little of the syrup with a spoon and drop it into a bowl of very cold water. If it forms a ball, it has reached the right temperature for making Italian meringue or a butter cream, for example. If the ball feels soft between your fingers, the syrup is less hot than if the ball feels hard. Ideally, you want a hard ball but since the sugar goes from one stage to the next very quickly it is better to use the sugar as soon as you see the ball form to avoid the risk of overcooking the sugar, which then becomes extremely difficult to work.

BLIND BAKE

This term refers to the partial or complete baking of a pastry shell before it is filled. This precooking stage prevents the pastry from becoming soft by its filling or by fruits that are subsequently added.

BOIL/SIMMER

A dish is "boiling" when it is placed over a high heat and large bubbles appear on the surface. This represents a higher temperature than when it is "simmering," which is when only small bubbles form on the surface.

BUTTER

Unless stated otherwise, the butter used in these recipes is sweet.

CARAMEL

Caramel is what is produced when white sugar is cooked beyond the stages where it is no longer a syrup.

To make this safely you must use a saucepan with a heavy base, because the pan needs to be able to withstand the very high temperatures needed for making caramel, and because a thick base will also ensure the heat diffuses more evenly. Pour in the water first, then the sugar. Never use more than one-third the weight of water to the weight of sugar (so, for ⅓ cup of sugar use no more than 2 tablespoons water). Place over a steady medium heat. Dissolve the sugar using a hand whisk, taking care not to flick the mixture up the sides of the pan. Bring to the boil when the sugar has dissolved, never before (because if the sugar is still solid when it boils it will not subsequently dissolve). Leave the syrup to concentrate without touching the pan. Beyond 300°F it will change to a caramel; it will start to take on color.

To stop the cooking, you must remove the pan from the heat a few seconds before the required color is achieved (the caramel will continue to color off the heat), or plunge the base of the pan into cold water for a few seconds. This second method is less preferable because the caramel cools and hence thickens, rendering it less workable than if it remains liquid.

COAGULATE, COAGULATION

Coagulation occurs when certain components of some liquid ingredients bind together to form a denser mass.

In baking, this can sometimes occur when heating eggs, which is why they should be cooked very gently. It rarely produces a required effect because coagulation of one ingredient (eggs, for example) is not desirable in the final dish (for instance an egg custard); it will be grainy and unevenly blended.

COAT, COATING

A coating is when a liquid achieves a consistency (mostly as a result of heating) sufficiently thick to coat the surface of an object that has been dipped in it. A spoon, for example, is no longer visible through the coating and is evenly covered by it. When cooking is involved, as in making custard or lemon curd, the coating has reached the desired thickness when you can draw a line through the coating on the back of a spoon and the line remains visible.

COLOR, COLORATION

This stage in cooking shows the change from the initial color of a dish to another under the effect of heat. Coloration occurs as soon as the initial color changes to another; it can go from a very light golden to a very dark brown.

CRUMBS (RUBBING-IN METHOD)

"Crumbs" are made by rubbing small pieces of butter into flour with your fingertips. This action means every grain of flour becomes coated in butter so that, little by little, you produce a pale colored mixture in which only tiny pieces of butter remain. To prevent the butter becoming warm, this rubbing in is done above the flour and butter in the bowl; by lifting and letting the crumbs fall you are introducing air and so cooling the mix.

You can also make the crumbs in a food mixer fitted with a blade. Put the flour and the cold cubed butter into the bowl and pulse for a few seconds. Next add the egg–water mixture in which the salt and sugar have been dissolved. Pulse the food mixer again, just until the dough forms. Turn out onto the counter top and knead a little with your palm then finish the preparation following the recipe.

EGGS

All these recipes use large eggs that weigh about 3 oz in the shell or 2½ oz out of the shell.

In cases where it may be necessary to halve the quantity of ingredients, you might need to divide a single egg in two. This is much easier if you break the egg, beat it, then use half only. For real precision, you can weigh the beaten egg using electronic scales: half a large egg weighs just over 1 oz.

Contrary to received wisdom, you should not whip egg whites until they are really firm if you need to combine them with other ingredients. In effect, stiffly whipped meringue tends to form lumps which are difficult to incorporate, and the extra mixing that stirring them in implies has the effect of causing the meringue to collapse. It is therefore much better, especially for making chocolate mousse, to whip egg whites until they are just supple, not firm. Then, work the whites in using a flexible spatula. This gentle action "relaxes" the whites and breaks down any lumps that may be present.

ELECTRONIC SCALES

A set of electronic scales is a useful aid for baking (along with a flexible spatula and plastic wrap) because it is possible to measure the smallest quantities (as well as large ones, naturally). Even an extra pinch of salt or baking powder can be all too apparent in the taste and the texture of the final product.

FLEXIBLE SPATULA

A "maryse" is the term used by French chefs to designate a flexible spatula made from rubber, plastic, or silicone. This utensil is one of the indispensable trio (along with electronic scales and plastic wrap) used in baking. It allows you to scrape the bowl perfectly clean, for example when you need to empty the contents of one to combine with the contents of another. In baking terms, every carefully measured ingredient counts (see under Electronic scales) and, by using this type of spatula, you don't leave any on the sides of the bowl. The flexibility of the spatula also allows you to delicately combine most preparations, especially those that include whisked egg whites (see Eggs) or flour (see Mixture). No other baking utensil performs this task so ably.

FLOUR, FLOURING

When you roll out pastry, you need to regularly flour the counter top or pastry board to prevent the pastry from sticking, while avoiding too much flour being incorporated in the dough. To effect this, scatter several pinches of flour on the counter top or board.

FLOUR TYPES

In baking terms, all-purpose flour is generally reserved for bread-style cakes (banana bread, pancakes, gingerbread, and so forth) where the final result has a crust and a soft interior. Baking powder and/or baking soda is sifted in with the flour. Self-rising flour is used for lighter cakes. It is worth seeking out the varieties sold as "super-sifted" or "superfine," which are presifted to ensure the grains are as fine and even as possible.

HOMOGENOUS

A preparation is "homogenous" when it is even in texture. That does not necessarily mean smooth: a homogenous texture can be grainy, but it must be uniformly grainy. When a smooth texture is required, this is specified in the recipe.

MIXTURE, MIXING

Most baking recipes use the following basic method: the dry ingredients are mixed together in one bowl, the liquid ingredients combined in another, then the two are brought together.

The mixing of dry ingredients rarely poses any problem (provided that the ingredients are correctly measured and the flour sifted); you can even prepare this stage in advance and keep the dry mixture for a day or two in a plastic bag or sealed box.

The mixing of liquids, however, can become a more delicate undertaking since the ingredients often have different temperatures (for example, melted butter that is still hot, eggs or milk taken directly from the fridge) or the temperature of one ingredient can affect another (melted butter will set if it is poured into cold milk), and this works against achieving a good mix. For this reason it is important that the temperature of liquid ingredients is the same before they are combined.

• To warm up an egg, plunge it for 1–2 minutes in a bowl filled with hot water.

• To warm up milk, put it in a saucepan over a gentle heat.

• To cool melted butter, pour it into a cold bowl.

Mixing the dry and wet ingredients represents another delicate stage in the baking process. This is the point at which the baking powder is activated, but its rising action does not last very long. Immediately dry and liquid ingredients are combined, the dish must be transferred to the oven. Furthermore, when flour comes into contact with a liquid and is worked with a utensil, the all-important "web" of gluten develops which is so essential to the structure of the dough or batter. On the other hand, if this gluten network is overdeveloped, the cake can be transformed into a stone. For this reason it is often specified that you do not use an electric whisk to mix wet and dry ingredients; instead the recommendation is to work the batter gently and as little as possible using a flexible spatula.

PIPING BAG, PIPING

A cone-shaped washable bag, usually with a set of nozzles of different sizes and shapes, is invaluable for making attractive individual buns or meringues on a baking sheet. It is also used for filling choux buns or for decorating the top of cakes with cream.

To fill the bag, start by sliding the nozzle into the base of the bag then block the nozzle by pushing a fold of the bag inside it. If you are right-handed, hold the bag in your left hand and fold back the top of the bag over your hand. Fill the bag with your free hand. Close the bag by turning it the other way up (nozzle pointing up) and twisting the end of the bag until the mixture starts to appear out of the nozzle. Squeeze to make the mixture ooze out and keep twisting the bag so that it is always tight.

PLASTIC WRAP

Plastic wrap, or cellophane, is an indispensable item in cake-baking (along with the flexible spatula and a set of electronic scales). It forms a barrier between the prepared dish and the air, one that protects it from oxidation and its consequences: drying out (hence a crust or skin), color change, microbial contamination…

Some professionals "contact seal" all their prepared dishes, meaning that plastic wrap is placed directly on the surface of the dish. In this book, this technique is above all recommended for the Pastry Cream (recipe 02), which tends to form a skin at the end of cooking. In most other cases, it is enough to stretch the plastic wrap over the top of the container in which the dish is prepared.

POMADE

In baking terms, a pomade is the term for butter which is supple in texture but still remains a little firm. This texture makes it easier to blend with other ingredients without it losing its structure (unlike melted butter), and also to beat it until light and fluffy.

There are two ways of achieving a pomade. Start by cutting the butter into small pieces so that it warms up more quickly and uniformly.

Method one: Leave the butter at room temperature until you can push your finger into it easily; this can take anything from 20 minutes to several hours depending on the temperature of the room.

Method two: Put the chopped butter in a heat-resistant bowl and place over a saucepan of boiling water that you have just removed from the heat. Leave the bowl above the heat source for a few seconds then remove and work the butter with a spatula until it forms a "pomade." If it proves hard work, place over the pan for a few more seconds.

ROLL OUT, ROLLING

This refers to pastry being rolled out using a rolling pin on a floured surface to the required size and thickness. The task of rolling out pastry evenly is easier if it is lifted and turned between each pass with the rolling pin. To ensure that the pastry doesn't stick to the work surface it should be lightly floured (see Flouring). You can also turn the pastry over at regular intervals and even up the edges with your fingers to achieve the required shape.

To divide a block in two, you need to roll the pastry out as a rectangle thin enough to be folded over then cut it with a sharp knife at the point of the fold.

To correctly position a circular pastry sheet in the tin, fold it in on itself twice to form a fan shape then place the point of the triangle on the centre of the tin. Unfold the sheet again and line the tin with the pastry, pressing it well into the angles and sides.

SIFT, SIFTING

Sifting flour removes any lumps by passing it through a strainer or fine sieve. You are strongly advised to sift your flour through a fine-mesh sieve for most if not all of these recipes, and it is well worth buying superfine flour, which is already sifted.

SIPHON

A siphon is an aluminum bottle that contains pressurized liquid gas. By activating the pump that controls the flow of the liquid up through a tube, the liquid is carbonated and so comes out in the form of mousse. This device allows you to transform sweetened liquid cream instantly into Chantilly.

WATER BATH

Using a water bath is a method of cooking that allows a dish to be heated more gently than is possible by exposing it directly to the heat source. This gentle cooking is achieved by placing the cake pan or mold inside another, larger, pan that contains boiling water.

Cooking with a water bath also prevents a dish from drying out. Once in the hot oven the water evaporates, continuously producing vapor and keeping the heat moist. For this purpose, there is no need to sit the dish directly in the water bath: you can put a shallow tray or pan under the rack on which you intend to cook your dish. The water bath should be placed in the oven when you preheat it. Then, when you are ready to cook, pour in the equivalent of a small saucepan of very hot water into the shallow tray.

Using a water bath is also a good way to defrost frozen fruit. Place the fruit in a bowl and cover with plastic wrap. Put the bowl on top of a pan of boiling water and leave for the required time (about 10 minutes for red fruit), stirring midway through. Defrosting by this method means that the fruits retain their color and their juice as they defrost.

Sometimes a recipe calls for ingredients to be chilled very quickly as, for example, when making Chantilly cream (see recipe 14). An ice-cold water bath is made by filling a bowl larger than your mixing bowl with ice cubes and very cold water. The mixing bowl is then plunged into this bath to chill the contents.

TABLE OF CONTENTS

1

CREAMS & CO.

CREAMS

Vanilla custard 01
Pastry cream 02
Butter cream 03
Almond cream 04
Lemon curd 05
Chocolate mousse 06
Chocolate ganache 07
Panna cotta 08

SAUCES & TOPPINGS

Caramel 09
Salty butter caramel sauce 10
Chocolate sauce 11
Red berry coulis 12
Red berry compote 13
Chantilly cream 14
Plain frosting 15
Chocolate frosting 16

2

SIMPLE CAKES

CLASSIC CAKES

Yogurt cake 17
Butter cake 18
Marbled cake 19

CHOCOLATE CAKES

Chocolate fondants 20
Flour-free chocolate cake 21
Brownies 22
Chocolate truffle cake 23

MADE IN THE U.S.

Carrot cake 24
Banana & walnut bread 25
Gingerbread 26
Corn bread 27

3

LAYERED CAKES

CHOUX PASTRY

Choux pastry 28
Praline choux 29
Caramel glaze 30
Profiteroles 31
Chocolate eclairs 32
Choux puffs 33
Rose St-Honoré choux 34

PUFF PASTRY

Puff pastry 35
Mille-feuilles 36
Kings' cake 37

CHEESECAKES

Tiramisu 38
Mascarpone cheesecake 39
Corsican cheesecake 40

FILLED CAKES

Jelly roll 41
Coffee log 42
Poppyseed cake 43
Chocolate charlotte 44
Vacherin 45

4

LITTLE CAKES

French meringues 46
Blueberry muffins 47
Chocolate muffins 48
Banana muffins 49
Bran & raisin muffins 50
Oat & apple muffins 51
Madeleines 52
Chocolate macaroons 53
Raspberry macaroons 54
Caramel macaroons 55
Star buns 56
Doughnuts 57
Maple syrup glaze 58
Chocolate chip cookies 59
Almost Oreos® 60
Biscuits 61
Pecan cookies 62
Breton cookies 63
Blueberry pancakes 64
Eggy bread 65

5

TARTS

Sweet pie pastry 66
Tarte tatin 67
Custard tart 68
Lemon meringue pie 69
Kiwi & mascarpone tartlets 70
Strawberry tartlets 71

INDEX OF RECIPES

Note: This index is organized by recipe number.

A

Almond cream 04
Almost Oreos® 60

B

Banana & walnut bread 25
Banana muffins 49
Biscuits 61
Blueberry muffins 47
Blueberry pancakes 64
Bran & raisin muffins 50
Breton biscuits 63
Brownies 22
Butter cake 18
Butter cream 03

C

Caramel 09
Caramel glaze 30
Caramel macaroons 55
Carrot cake 24
Chantilly cream 14
Chocolate charlotte 44
Chocolate chip cookies 59
Chocolate eclairs 32
Chocolate fondants 20
Chocolate frosting 16
Chocolate ganache 07
Chocolate macaroons 53
Chocolate mousse 06
Chocolate muffins 48
Chocolate sauce 11
Chocolate truffle cake 23
Choux pastry 28
Choux puffs 33
Coffee log 42
Corn bread 27
Corsican cheesecake 40
Custard tart 68

D

Doughnuts 57

E

Eggy bread 65

F

Flour-free chocolate cake 21
French meringues 46

G

Gingerbread 26

J

Jelly roll 41

K

Kings' cake 37
Kiwi & mascarpone tartlets . . . 70

L

Lemon curd 05
Lemon meringue pie 69

M

Madeleines 52
Maple syrup glaze 58
Marbled cake 19
Mascarpone cheesecake 39
Mille-feuilles 36

O

Oat & apple muffins 51

P

Panna cotta 08
Pastry cream 02
Pecan cookies 62
Plain frosting 15
Poppyseed cake 43
Praline choux 29
Profiteroles 31
Puff pastry 35

R

Raspberry macaroons 54
Red berry compote 13
Red berry coulis 12
Rose St-Honoré choux 34

S

Salty butter caramel sauce 10
Star buns 56
Strawberry tartlets 71
Sweet pie pastry 66

T

Tarte tatin 67
Tiramisu 38

V

Vacherin 45
Vanilla custard 01

Y

Yogurt cake 17

INDEX BY INGREDIENTS

Note: This index is organized by recipe number.

A

almonds
- Almond cream 04
- Chocolate macaroons 53
- Flour-free chocolate cake 21
- Kings' cake 37
- Poppyseed cake 43
- Strawberry tartlets 71

apples
- Oat & apple muffins 51
- Tarte tatin 67

B

bananas
- Banana & walnut bread 25
- Banana muffins 49

blueberries
- Blueberry muffins 47
- Blueberry pancakes 64

bread
- Banana & walnut bread 25
- Corn bread 27
- Gingerbread 26

butter
- Almond cream 04
- Breton cookies 63
- Butter cake 18
- Butter cream 03
- Chocolate frosting 16
- Coffee log 42
- Madeleines 52
- Salty butter caramel sauce 10

C

caramel
- Basic recipe 09
- Caramel macaroons 55
- Caramel glaze 30
- Salty butter caramel sauce 10

cereals
- Bran & raisin muffins 50
- Oat & apple muffins 51

chantilly cream
- Basic recipe 14
- Mille-feuilles 36
- Rose St-Honoré choux 34
- Vacherin 45

cheesecakes
- Corsican cheesecake 40
- Mascarpone cheesecake 39

chocolate
- Almost Oreos® 60
- Brownies 22
- Chocolate charlotte 44
- Chocolate chip cookies 59
- Chocolate eclairs 32
- Chocolate fondants 20
- Chocolate frosting 16
- Chocolate ganache 07
- Chocolate macaroons 53
- Chocolate mousse 06
- Chocolate muffins 48
- Chocolate sauce 11
- Chocolate truffle cake 23
- Flour-free chocolate cake 21
- Marbled cake 19
- Profiteroles 31

choux pastry
- Basic recipe 28
- Caramel glaze 30
- Chocolate eclairs 32
- Choux puffs 33
- Praline choux 29
- Profiteroles 31
- Rose St-Honoré choux 34

coffee
- Butter cream 03
- Coffee log 42
- Tiramisu 38

cookies
- Almost Oreos® 60
- Breton cookies 63
- Chocolate chip cookies 59
- Pecan cookies 62

creams
- Almond cream 04
- Butter cream 03
- Chantilly cream 14
- Pastry cream 02

custard
- Custard tart 68
- Vanilla custard 01

D

dried fruit
- Biscuits 61
- Bran & raisin muffins 50
- Carrot cake 24

F

frosting
- Caramel glaze 30
- Carrot cake frosting 24
- Chocolate eclairs 32
- Chocolate frosting 16
- Maple syrup glaze 58
- Plain frosting 15
- Rose St-Honoré choux 34

fruit
- Banana & walnut bread 25
- Banana muffins 49
- Blueberry muffins 47
- Blueberry pancakes 64
- Kiwi & mascarpone tartlets 70

Lemon curd 05
Lemon meringue pie 69
Oat & apple muffins 51
Raspberry macaroons 54
Red berry compote 13
Red berry coulis 12
Strawberry tartlets 71
Tarte tatin 67
Vacherin 45

L

lemon
Corsican cheesecake 40
Lemon curd 05
Lemon meringue pie 69
Yogurt cake 17

M

macaroons
Caramel macaroons 55
Chocolate macaroons 53
Raspberry macaroons 54
mascarpone
Kiwi & mascarpone tartlets 70
Mascarpone cheesecake 39
Tiramisu 38
meringue
French meringues 46
Lemon meringue pie 69
Vacherin 45
mousse, chocolate
Basic recipe 06
Chocolate charlotte 44
muffins
Banana muffins 49
Blueberry muffins 47
Bran & raisin muffins 50
Chocolate muffins 48
Oat & apple muffins 51

N

nuts
Banana & walnut bread 25
Brownies 22
Carrot cake 24
Pecan cookies 62

P

pastry
Choux pastry 28
Puff pastry 35
Sweet pie pastry 66
pastry cream
Basic recipe 02
Chocolate eclairs 32
Kings' cake 37
Mille-feuilles 36
Rose St-Honoré choux 34
puff pastry
Basic recipe 35
Kings' cake 37
Mille-feuilles 36

R

red berries
Red berry coulis 12
Red berry compote 13

S

sauces
Chocolate sauce 11
Salty butter caramel sauce 10
Vanilla custard 01
spices
Carrot cake 24
Doughnuts 57
Gingerbread 26
strawberries
Biscuits 61
Eggy bread 65
Strawberry tartlets 71
sweet pie pastry
Basic recipe 66
Custard tart 68
Lemon meringue pie 69
Strawberry tartlets 71
Tarte tatin 67

T

tarts
Custard tart 68
Kiwi & mascarpone tartlets 70
Lemon meringue pie 69
Strawberry tartlets 71
Tarte tatin 67

V

vanilla
Banana & walnut bread 25
Butter cake 18
Butter cream 03
Chantilly cream 14
Chocolate chip cookies 59
Custard tart 68
Jelly roll 41
Madeleines 52
Mascarpone cheesecake 39
Panna cotta 08
Star buns 56
Vanilla custard 01

W

walnuts
Banana & walnut bread 25

ACKNOWLEDGMENTS

My thanks to Emmanuel Le Vallois for his confidence in this project.

Also to Sonia and Fred Lucano for their superb work and for their encouragement when I needed it.

Thanks too to Rose-Marie Di Domenico for her tactful management of the work.

Thanks to Jérôme, for his help (lots of washing up!) and for tasting all the baking I presented him with at any hour of the day or night...

Finally, my thanks to Véronique Magnier for the books and recipes I inherited from her.

The author and publishers wish to thank Magimix for the loan of a mixer.
www.magimix.com

Props: Emmanuelle Javelle
Design: Alexandre Nicolas
English translation and adaptation: JMS Books llp
Layout: cbdesign